NEW DIRECTIONS FOR ADULT AND CONTINUING EDUCATION

Susan Imel, *Ohio State University*
EDITOR-IN-CHIEF

Charting a Course for Continuing Professional Education: Reframing Professional Practice

Vivian W. Mott
East Carolina University

Barbara J. Daley
University of Wisconsin—Milwaukee

EDITORS

Number 86, Summer 2000

JOSSEY-BASS PUBLISHERS
San Francisco

CHARTING A COURSE FOR CONTINUING PROFESSIONAL EDUCATION:
REFRAMING PROFESSIONAL PRACTICE
Vivian W. Mott, Barbara J. Daley (eds.)
New Directions for Adult and Continuing Education, no. 86
Susan Imel, Editor-in-Chief

Microfilm copies of issues and articles are available in 16mm and 35mm, as well as microfiche in 105mm, through University Microfilms Inc., 300 North Zeeb Road, Ann Arbor, Michigan 48106-1346.

ISSN 1052-2891   ISBN 0-7879-5424-1

NEW DIRECTIONS FOR ADULT AND CONTINUING EDUCATION is part of The Jossey-Bass Higher and Adult Education Series and is published quarterly by Jossey-Bass Inc., Publishers, 350 Sansome Street, San Francisco, California 94104-1342. Periodicals postage paid at San Francisco, California, and at additional mailing offices. Postmaster: Send address changes to New Directions for Adult and Continuing Education, Jossey-Bass Inc., Publishers, 350 Sansome Street, San Francisco, California 94104-1342.

SUBSCRIPTIONS cost $58.00 for individuals and $104.00 for institutions, agencies, and libraries.

EDITORIAL CORRESPONDENCE should be sent to the Editor-in-Chief, Susan Imel, ERIC/ACVE, 1900 Kenny Road, Columbus, Ohio 43210-1090. E-mail: imel.1@osu.edu.

Cover photograph by Wernher Krutein/PHOTOVAULT © 1990.

www.josseybass.com

Printed in the United States of America on acid-free recycled paper containing 100 percent recovered waste paper, of which at least 20 percent is postconsumer waste.

CONTENTS

Editors' Notes

Continuing professional education (CPE) has undergone significant change in the past decades, yet there is little current literature that assists practitioners in developing an expanded understanding of the new issues, developing trends, and future needs of this important segment of adult education. In his classic text, *Continuing Learning in the Professions*, Houle (1980) states, "The task for this generation is to move ahead as creatively as possible, amid all the distractions and complexities of practice to aid professions . . . constantly to refine their sensitiveness, enlarge their concepts, add to their knowledge, and perfect their skills so that they can discharge their responsibilities within the context of their own personalities and the needs of the society of which they are collectively a part" (p. 316). Even though these words were written twenty years ago, the need still exists for CPE to move ahead creatively as a field of practice. In many ways, the field of CPE is even more fragmented now than in Houle's conceptualization. CPE providers tend to identify with and practice within their individual professions rather than within the general field of adult education. Yet there is a great deal that CPE providers can learn collaboratively from each other, regardless of the specific profession to which they belong.

The intent of this volume is to provide a resource for practitioners to help set new directions for the field of CPE across multiple professions. The chapters in this issue of *New Directions for Adult and Continuing Education* are organized in three parts that provide a brief review of the development of the field of CPE, analyze significant issues and trends that are shaping and changing the field, and propose a vision of the future of CPE.

In the first part, Ronald M. Cervero (Chapter One) examines the development of CPE and discusses trends and issues currently shaping the field. Cervero analyzes how workplace education, distance education, collaborative practices, and regulatory agencies are shaping current practices. He then identifies critical issues that must be addressed in building new creative systems of continuing education. Alan B. Knox (Chapter Two) adds to this discussion by exploring the linkages and connections between preprofessional and continuing professional education. He indicates that new systems of CPE must include greater integration of preprofessional and continuing professional education, offers guidelines for practitioners to develop these connections, and suggests two critical future issues to consider.

The second part analyzes issues and trends within the field of CPE. Vivian W. Mott (Chapter Three) explores the rise of CPE, providers, and concepts of learning in the workplace. The chapter focuses on models that facilitate the development of professional expertise and suggests a new model of learning in and from the workplace. Barbara J. Daley (Chapter Four) then offers a new way to understand how professionals learn within the context of their professional practice. She explains the process by which professionals construct a knowledge base in the context of their practice, yet change that knowledge base on the basis of new meaning derived from professional experiences. Judith M. Ottoson (Chapter Five) challenges the field of CPE to begin developing a unique evaluation theory that can be applied in the practice of CPE. Drawing from cross-disciplinary evaluation theory, she identifies practical methods by which practitioners can conduct comprehensive program evaluation for the purpose of improving professional service. Ruth F. Craven and Martha B. DuHamel (Chapter Six) outline how the interplay between program planning and marketing is essential for CPE providers in highly competitive markets. Craven and DuHamel offer practical approaches to marketing based on their extensive experiences in the field of CPE. Finally, Patricia Ann Lawler (Chapter Seven) presents her view on ethics in CPE. Ethical issues, ethical decision making, and actual cases from CPE are used in this chapter to help practitioners uncover the subtle yet pervasive ethical issues within the CPE practice.

The final part focuses on setting future directions for the practice of CPE. Arthur L. Wilson (Chapter Eight) challenges CPE providers to understand professional practice in a new way. He argues that professionals are losing decision-making authority and professional autonomy as systems rather than individuals assume control of professional practice. He challenges CPE providers to take a direct role in reshaping these changing dynamics. Finally, Barbara Daley and Vivian Mott (Chapter Nine) synthesize information from the preceding eight chapters and propose a reframed vision for the field of CPE. The proposed vision changes the role of CPE provider from providing program content to improving professional practice through the delivery of education, evaluation, and consultation.

We believe that this overview of CPE development, trends, issues, and future vision can lay the groundwork for practitioners to examine their practice and, as Houle advocated, "move ahead as creatively as possible" (1980, p. 316).

Vivian W. Mott
Barbara J. Daley
Editors

Reference

Houle, C. O. Continuing Learning in the Professions. San Francisco: Jossey-Bass, 1980.

VIVIAN W. MOTT is assistant professor in the Department of Counselor and Adult Education, East Carolina University, Greenville, North Carolina.

BARBARA J. DALEY is assistant professor of adult and continuing education in the Department of Administrative Leadership at the University of Wisconsin–Milwaukee.

1

Compared to the initial stages of professional education, systems of continuing education for the professions are in their infancy. In this chapter, four trends and three issues shaping the future of continuing education are identified.

Trends and Issues in Continuing Professional Education

Ronald M. Cervero

A central feature of North American societies in the twentieth century has been the professionalization of their workforces. One estimate is that nearly 25 percent of the American workforce claims membership in a profession (Cervero, 1988). These professionals teach our children, guide our businesses, manage and account for our money, settle our civil disputes, diagnose and treat our mental and physical ills, fight our wars, and help mediate our relationships with God. Thus it is important to keep our eyes on what is truly at stake in continuing education. The bottom line of continuing education is to improve the practice of these teachers, physicians, managers, and clergy. It is instructive to contrast this bottom line with the picture of the most frequently encountered form of continuing education: "It is dominated by the informational update. In what is typically an intensive two- or three-day short course, a single instructor lectures and lectures and lectures fairly large groups of business and professional people, who sit for long hours in an audiovisual twilight, making never-to-be-read notes at rows of narrow tables covered with green baize and appointed with fat binders and sweating pictures of ice water" (Nowlen, 1988, p. 23). This picture is as universally recognizable to people in any profession as it is criticized for being largely ineffective in improving the performance of these same professionals. Indeed, the familiarity of this picture would be funny if the importance of continuing education were not so great.

A version of this chapter was originally presented at the Institute for Professional Development, University of Alberta.

Roots and Development of Continuing Professional Education

An incredible amount of resources, both financial and human, are used to support the three to six years of professionals' initial education. Until recently, however, little systematic thought was given to what happens for the following forty years of professional practice. Many leaders in the professions believed that these years of preservice professional education, along with some refreshers, were sufficient for a lifetime of work. However, with rapid social changes (see Wilson, Chapter Eight, this volume), the explosion of research-based knowledge, and technological innovations, many of these leaders now understand the need to prepare people continually through continuing education for forty years of professional practice (Houle, 1980).

Beginning in the 1960s, we began to see embryonic evidence for systems of continuing education. Perhaps the first clear signal of this new view was the publication in 1962 of a conceptual scheme for the lifelong education of physicians (Dryer, 1962). The 1970s saw the beginning of what is now widespread use of continuing education as a basis for relicensure and recertification (Cervero and Azzaretto, 1990). By the 1980s, organized and comprehensive programs of continuing education were developed in engineering, accounting, law, medicine, pharmacy, veterinary medicine, social work, librarianship, architecture, nursing home administration, nursing, management, public school education, and many other professions (Cervero, 1988). During that decade, many professions developed their systems of accreditation for providers of continuing education (Kenny, 1985).

As we near the end of the 1990s, the picture of a single instructor lecturing large groups of professionals is still easily recognizable as the predominant form of continuing education. We do not yet have a similarly recognizable picture of a system of continuing education that is effective in today's complex world. The major reason for this lack of a unifying picture of effective continuing education is that the professions are in a transitional stage, experimenting with many different purposes, forms, and institutional locations for the delivery of continuing education. These systems, such as they are, are incredibly primitive. I would characterize them as *devoted mainly to updating practitioners about the newest developments, which are transmitted in a didactic fashion and offered by a pluralistic group of providers (workplaces, for-profits, and universities) that do not work together in any coordinated fashion.* Relatively speaking, these systems of continuing education are in their infancy. By way of analogy, at the end of the twentieth century continuing education is in the same state of development as preservice education was at the beginning of the century. Medical education serves as a useful point of comparison. In his 1910 report on medical schools in Canada and the United States, Abraham Flexner found that only 16 of 155 schools expected that their incoming students would have any previous college education, and he recommended closing the schools that did not. It is unlikely that anyone in 1910 would have predicted the structure of medical education today. Likewise, systems of continuing education will grow through this transitional period to achieve coherence, size, and stature equivalent to those of the preservice stage of professional education. Indeed, the leaders of most professions would probably agree that "what we hardly dare prophesy today will be seen by later generations as efforts to achieve a manifest necessity" (Houle, 1980, p. 302). While these systems of continuing education are in transition (Young, 1998), many choices must be made. The remainder of this chapter describes four emerging trends and three critical issues that must be addressed in building these systems of continuing education for the professions.

Four Trends in the 1990s

Four trends have changed the face of continuing professional education in the 1990s.

TREND 1. *The amount of continuing education offered at the workplace dwarfs that offered by any other type of provider, and surpasses that of all other providers combined.*

Employers such as businesses, hospitals, social service agencies, and government offer a tremendous amount of education to their employees. In 1996, $60 billion was spent on providing formal education to 59 million people in the United States, the majority of whom were professionals and middle and upper management ("A Statistical Picture. . .," 1997). The corporate average spent on employee education is about 1.5 percent of payroll and 1 percent of gross revenues. The consensus among observers is that these figures grossly underestimate both the amount of dollars spent and the number of people trained. The amount spent on employee education would be about $210 billion if indirect costs, such as wages while studying, and fixed costs, such as building construction, were included. The estimated number of people attending programs accounts for only formal education and says nothing about the nonformal on-the-job training that is universal in work settings.

Some corporations, especially those that employ many professionals, are particularly education intensive (Davis and Botkin, 1994). For example, Arthur Anderson, a $5 billion accounting and consulting firm, spends more than $300 million, which was 6.5 percent of 1992 revenues. This is comparable to the University of Virginia's budget and larger than the budgets of Purdue and Syracuse Universities. Motorola spends $120 million, or 3.6 percent of its payroll. Finally, if the education arms of General Electric, AT&T, or IBM were spun off as public universities, their revenues would exceed the budgets of either Ohio State University or the University of Michigan.

TREND 2. *Universities and professional associations are active and important providers, with an increasing number of programs being offered in distance education formats.*

Nearly every university sponsors continuing education programs either through its various professional schools, such as medicine, social work, and engineering, or through a university-wide continuing education unit. Significant growth is under way in the amount of continuing education offered by universities. The Council on Graduate Schools reports, "In particular, certificate programs, which issue documents of completion and sometimes an accreditation to students who have completed a specified course of study, are growing in enrollments by about 20 percent annually" (Koss-Feder, 1998, p. 4).

The major growth area is, without a doubt, in distance learning programs. There are 1,200 degree and certificate distance learning programs offered by 900 accredited colleges (Koss-Feder, 1998). For example, Western Governors University (WGU), a completely virtual college based in Salt Lake City and Denver, offered its first courses in 1998. Started by governors from eighteen Western states and encompassing the state universities in those areas, WGU initially offered continuing education courses on the Web and on satellite TV. Students from all over the world are able to enroll in programs and courses that come from a range of sources, including corporations and universities. The state of California has privatized its virtual university, turning it into the California Virtual University Foundation, which includes the state's university systems and several high-tech companies, such as Sun Microsystems, Pacific Bell, and Oracle. The Virtual University provides students with a choice of 1,600 courses and 100 complete degree or certificate programs, all of which are available entirely on-line ("California Spins . . .," 1998).

Professional associations are also major providers of continuing education. In fact, education is a major if not the primary function of associations. More than five thousand American and Canadian associations and many more state, provincial, and local associations are either organized independently or affiliated with the national body. A recent study of 5,500 national associations by the Hudson Institute on behalf of the American Society of Association Executives (Maurer and Sheets, 1998) found that 90 percent of associations offer continuing education to their members and the public. They spend $8.5 billion to offer courses on technical and scientific matters and business practices.

TREND 3. *There are an increasing number of collaborative arrangements among providers, especially between universities and workplaces.*

One movement that has accelerated in the past decade is that public universities are under great pressure to play a larger role in the economic development of their state or region. Continuing education is clearly part of the economic development strategy, so universities and businesses are actively collaborating in structuring continuing education programs. For example, about 90 percent of the education that employers offer to professionals, executives, and middle managers is developed through collaborative arrangements, as opposed to using only in-house staff ("A Statistical Picture...," 1997). Studies of universities and professional schools (Cervero, 1988, 1992) have found that anywhere from 60 to 85 percent of their programs involve some form of collaboration. Similar surveys have found that about 50 percent of professional associations and 85 percent of independent providers engage in collaborative programming. For example, "an increasing number of companies are customizing courses for their employees in conjunction with major universities. The former Coopers & Lybrand in the newly named PricewaterhouseCoopers, for example, has offered three-day and five-day executive education for its partners at Dartmouth's Amos Tuck School of Business Administration and the Harvard Business School" (Koss-Feder, 1998, p. 3).

These collaborative efforts are not limited to universities and businesses. In the early 1990s, the Dupont Corporation contracted all of its training and development to the Forum Corporation, spending between $300 to $500 million a year. Corporate executives felt they were spending too much money, the quality was variable, and there was lots of duplication and no way of measuring impact. They also believed that training was not a core competence for them and that they should contract it out to a global player. Davis and Botkin (1994, p. 92) explain that "to lower its costs, Dupont moved training from a fixed to a variable cost so that training budgets became allocated to individual business units and weren't carried as corporate overhead. To raise quality, it repositioned training from a developmental tool for individuals to a strategic tool for the entire business."

TREND 4. *Continuing education is being used more frequently to regulate professionals' practice.*

The first three trends focus on the institutional provision of continuing education. However, continuing education touches individual professionals in many ways and is increasingly being used to regulate their practice. Perhaps the most obvious example is increased use of continuing education as a basis for relicensure. What started in the 1970s is now widespread such that "every profession, whether licensed or certified, uses some form of mandatory CE" (Collins, 1998b, p. 13). For example, the number of states requiring continuing education for relicensure has risen consistently for the past two decades: the number of states that certify public accountants increased from twenty states in 1976 to forty-nine today; the number that certify lawyers increased from ten to thirty-seven, and the number that certify pharmacists increased from fourteen to forty-seven.

There are also innumerable "voluntary" certification programs. In the securities industry, regulatory bodies such as the New York Stock Exchange now require mandatory CE for their employees (Collins, 1998b). All twenty-one medical specialty boards have recertification requirements that include continuing education. More professions are going to follow the example of the Royal College of Physicians and Surgeons of Canada, which has moved beyond the accumulation of hours of "seat time" for recertification. Its Maintenance of Competence Program allows physicians to use activities such as participation in audits of practice and a personal learning portfolio, which describes their significant learning during the past year. The portfolio describes the area of expertise "on which individuals have focused their continued learning and reflects the quality of their continuing professional development since initial certification by the Royal College" (Royal College of Physicians and Surgeons of Canada, 1995, p. 11).

Critical Issues for the Future of Continuing Education

The task of building systems of continuing education is fundamentally more complex than what faced leaders earlier in the twentieth century as they successfully built the existing systems of preservice professional education. Following are three critical issues that must be addressed in building systems of continuing education.

ISSUE 1. *Continuing education for what? The struggle between updating professionals' knowledge versus improving professional practice.*

The most fundamental question is, What is the problem for which continuing education is the answer? If the picture painted at the beginning of the chapter is the answer, then it is clear that the problem has been conceived as keeping professionals up to date on the profession's knowledge base. In fact, keeping professionals up to date is as close to a unifying aim as continuing education has (Nowlen, 1988). This educational model flows from the deeply embedded view that professional practice consists of instrumental problem solving made rigorous by the application of scientific theory and technique (Schön, 1987; see also Mott, Chapter Three, this volume). This scientific knowledge is produced by researchers, and the foundation is laid in professional school, with the additional building blocks added through forty years of continuing education. In a sense, continuing education becomes an extension of faculty members' lines of research. Yet most of the problems professionals face are not in the book. Schön's (1987, p. 3) studies of professional practice led him to say, "In the varied topography of professional practice, there is a high, hard ground overlooking a swamp. On the high ground, manageable problems lend themselves to solution through the application of research-based theory and technique. In the swampy lowland, messy, confusing problems defy technical solution. The

irony of this situation is that the problems of the high ground tend to be relatively unimportant to individuals or society at large . . . while in the swamp
lie the problems of greatest human concern."

What does it mean for education if we believe that professionals conduct most of their practice in the swamp of the real world? Some professional schools have begun moving to more problem-centered curricula
(Bok, 1984). However, continuing education has a great advantage over
other stages of professional education in seeking to promote effective practice. It occurs when professionals are most likely to be aware of a need for
better ways to think about what they do. But if we are to exploit this natural
advantage and move our systems beyond the update model, we need to find
better ways to integrate continuing education, both its content and its educational design, into the ongoing individual and collective practice of professionals (see Mott, Chapter Three, and Daley, Chapter Four, this volume).

ISSUE 2. *Who benefits from continuing education? The struggle between the
learning agenda and the political and economic agendas of continuing education.*

In a sense, this issue is also about the purposes of continuing education.
While the first issue dealt with the various educational purposes for continuing education, this issue recognizes the reality that continuing education is
about many things in addition to professionals' learning. I believe we all recognize that continuing education can and often does improve professionals'
knowledge and positively impacts our organizations and communities
(Umble and Cervero, 1996). However, continuing education also offers many
additional benefits to individuals and organizations. Any director of continuing education for a professional school recognizes the expectation to generate surplus revenues to be used to support faculty members' travel,
research, and instruction. Any director for a professional association knows
that programs need to generate revenues to fund staff salaries in nonrevenue-
producing activities, such as lobbying, maintaining certification programs,
and promoting the public image of the profession. Training programs are an
important benefit that can help to retain employees, as one survey found:
"Among the many benefits offered to their employees, continuing education
is considered the most important after health insurance. More than 90 percent of the companies surveyed currently offer CE as an employee benefit
and 97 percent plan to offer their employees this benefit by 2000" (University Continuing Education Association, 1998, p. 31).

There is no reason to expect that education can or even should be
immune from the political and economic agendas of our institutions and
the wider society (see Wilson, Chapter Eight, this volume). To address these
realities, the first question any institution needs to ask is, What is the mission of my institution and where does continuing education fit in that mission? The second question is, Whose interests will be served by offering

continuing education and what are those interests? Finally, What are the political relationships at my institution and how will they enable or constrain implementing the vision for continuing education? This struggle between the learning agenda and the political economic agenda will always exist. However, by answering these three questions, we will be better able to negotiate a successful resolution to this struggle (see Lawler, Chapter Seven, this volume).

ISSUE 3. *Who will provide continuing education? The struggle for turf versus collaborative relationships.*

Most continuing education is provided through some sort of collaboration between two or more institutions. A central finding of the body of research on this topic is that any understanding of collaboration for continuing education has to recognize the larger organizational goals being pursued through the formation of such relationships. For example, a study of collaborative programs in engineering (Colgan, 1989) found that although the respondents believed that the programs were needed to keep engineers up to date with the new technologies, the university-corporation relationship was driven by larger institutional issues. For corporations, the benefits included access to university students as prospective employees, and more direct and regular access to university faculty and research. For universities, the programs provided a mechanism to secure research contracts and faculty consulting, provided a means to secure student internships, and generated profits to subsidize other institutional functions. In a similar vein, other research (Cervero, 1984; Maclean, 1996) has found that a primary reason that medical schools have extensive collaborative relationships with community hospitals is to increase the number of patient referrals to the university hospital that result from faculty members speaking at these programs.

While there is general agreement that collaborative programming is a good, even "politically correct" idea, the central question is always, Who's in charge? This governance issue is always negotiated in partnerships, and the central issues typically revolve around who controls the content of the program and how profits and losses will be shared. Collaboration is a strategy that has been used extensively and that will continue to be used to develop systems of continuing education. However, astute leaders recognize that the formation of collaborative relationships is fundamentally a political process in which costs and benefits must be clearly weighed, including those involving organizational agendas other than those connected to the continuing education program. Thus, effective partnerships will develop not from a belief that collaboration is the right thing to do but from a definitive understanding of the goals to be achieved by the partnership, from a clear recognition of the benefits to be gained by each institution, and from the contribution of equivalent resources by each partner (Cervero, 1988; Collins, 1998a).

A Concluding Note

The leaders of workplaces, professional associations, universities, and governments have both a tremendous opportunity and a clear responsibility to further develop the systems of continuing education for the professions. These three issues illuminate the critical choices that are before institutional leaders and individual professionals in building these systems (see Daley and Mott, Chapter Nine, this volume). As with any human-constructed system, the building of a coordinated system of continuing education for any profession is a political process that will be marked by fundamental struggles over the educational agenda and over the competing interests of the educational agenda and the political-economic agendas of the multiple stakeholders in continuing education. Because it is a political process, then, it is crucial that all of the stakeholders participate in a substantive way in negotiating these agendas for continuing education, because the immediate and long-term negotiation of these struggles will define whether continuing education can make a demonstrable impact on the quality of professional practice.

References

Bok, D. "Needed: A New Way to Train Doctors." *Harvard Magazine,* May-June 1984, pp. 32–43, 70–71.

"California Spins Off Its Virtual U." *Techweb,* July 30, 1998, p. 1.

Cervero, R. M. "Collaboration in University Continuing Professional Education." In H. W. Beder (ed.), *Realizing the Potential of Interorganizational Cooperation.* New Directions for Continuing Education, no. 23. San Francisco: Jossey-Bass, 1984.

Cervero, R. M. *Effective Continuing Education for Professionals.* San Francisco: Jossey-Bass, 1988.

Cervero, R. M. "Cooperation and Collaboration in the Field of Continuing Professional Education." In E. S. Hunt (ed.), *Professional Workers as Learners.* Washington, D.C.: U.S. Department of Education, 1992.

Cervero, R. M., and Azzaretto, J. F. (eds.). *Visions for the Future of Continuing Professional Education.* Athens: Georgia Center for Continuing Education, University of Georgia, 1990.

Colgan, A. H. "Continuing Professional Education: A Study of Collaborative Relationships in Engineering Universities and Corporations." Unpublished doctoral dissertation, University of Illinois at Urbana-Champaign, 1989.

Collins, M. M. "Exploring Professional Associations' Perceptions of Institutions of Higher Education as Potential Partners." Unpublished doctoral dissertation, Pennsylvania State University, 1998a.

Collins, M. M. "An Interview with Louis Phillips." *Journal of Continuing Higher Education,* Spring 1998b, 12–18.

Davis, S., and Botkin, J. *The Monster Under the Bed: How Business Is Mastering the Opportunity of Knowledge for Profit.* New York: Simon & Schuster, 1994.

Dryer, B. V. "Lifetime Learning for Physicians: Principles, Practices, Proposals." *Journal of Medical Education,* 1962, 37, Part 2.

Flexner, A. *Medical Education in the United States and Canada.* New York: Carnegie Foundation for the Advancement of Teaching, 1910.

Houle, C. O. *Continuing Learning in the Professions.* San Francisco: Jossey-Bass, 1980.

Kenny, W. R. "Program Planning and Accreditation." In R. M. Cervero and C. L. Scanlan (eds.), *Problems and Prospects in Continuing Professional Education.* New Directions for Continuing Education, no. 27. San Francisco: Jossey-Bass, 1985.

Koss-Feder, L. "Brushing Up." *Time* (Special Issue), July 20, 1998.

Maclean, R. G. "Negotiating Between Competing Interests in Planning Continuing Medical Education." In R. M. Cervero and A. L. Wilson (eds.), *What Really Matters in Adult Education Program Planning: Lessons in Negotiating Power and Interests.* New Directions for Adult and Continuing Education, no. 69. San Francisco: Jossey-Bass, 1996.

Maurer, C., and Sheets, T. E. "Foreword to Volume 1, National Organizations of the U.S." *Encyclopedia of Associations.* (33rd ed.) Detroit: Gale Research, 1998.

Nowlen, P. M. *A New Approach to Continuing Education for Business and the Professions: The Performance Model.* Old Tappan, N.J.: Macmillan, 1988.

Royal College of Physicians and Surgeons of Canada. *Maintenance of Competence Program: A Program to Assist Fellows to Manage Their Professional Development.* Ottawa, Ontario: Royal College of Physicians and Surgeons of Canada, 1995.

Schön, D. A. *Educating the Reflective Practitioner: Toward a New Design for Teaching and Learning in the Professions.* San Francisco: Jossey-Bass, 1987.

"A Statistical Picture of Employer Sponsored Training in the United States." *Training,* Oct. 1997, pp. 34–70.

Umble, K. E., and Cervero, R. M. "Impact Studies in Continuing Education for Health Professionals: A Critique of the Research Syntheses." *Evaluation & the Health Professions,* 1996, *19*(2), 148–174.

University Continuing Education Association. *Lifelong Learning Trends: A Profile of Continuing Higher Education.* (5th ed.) Washington, D.C.: University Continuing Education Association, 1998.

Young, W. H. (ed). *Continuing Professional Education in Transition.* Malabar, Fla.: Krieger, 1998.

RONALD M. CERVERO *is professor of adult education at the University of Georgia in Athens, Georgia.*

2

*Those who plan and conduct preprofessional and continu-
ing professional education programs can use an understanding of the continuum to strengthen their current and
future programs.*

The Continuum of Professional
Education and Practice

Alan B. Knox

Developing a continuum of professional education has long been a challenge to continuing professional education (CPE) providers and their
counterparts within professional development programs. Occasional ref-
erences to this continuum belie the gulf that separates preprofessional
education and continuing professional education. As we move to creating
"systems of continuing education" (Cervero, Chapter One, this volume),
the linkages between CPE and preprofessional education take on greater
importance to CPE providers and to those educators who facilitate the
transition from preparatory education to practice.

   This chapter explores how an understanding of the continuum of
professional education can be used to strengthen both CPE and preprofessional programs. Following a brief reference to books and articles on
this topic and to the potential benefits of a comprehensive perspective on
this continuum, guidelines are then suggested that pertain to program
coordination, responsiveness to learners, encouraging application, and
stakeholder expectations. The chapter concludes with discussion of two
future directions—relations among providers and attention to research
and evaluation.

Themes and Benefits of the Continuum of
Professional Education

Themes on the professional education continuum have been developed in
a wide variety of the CPE literature. Many of these themes are included in
Houle's (1992) book on the literature of adult education. Houle's (1973)

NEW DIRECTIONS FOR ADULT AND CONTINUING EDUCATION, no. 86, Summer 2000   © Jossey-Bass Publishers

book on the external degree was an early chronicle of a transition central to the continuum that was occurring at that time. However, it is Houle's book *Continuing Learning in the Professions* (1980) that provides the most comprehensive overview of the continuum to date. More recent volumes by Cervero (1988); Cevero, Azzaretto, and Associates (1990); and Cervero and Scanlan (1985) provide useful refinements. Attention to the continuum of professional education has also occurred in specific professional fields (Adelson, Watkins, and Caplan, 1985; Manning and DeBakey, 1987; Nowlen, 1988). Millard's (1991) overview of higher education trends frequently addresses the continuum of preprofessional and continuing education, and a book by Duning, Van Kekerix, and Zaborowski (1993) explores the impact of instructional technology and distance education, which can strengthen the continuum. The continuum of professional education has both a personal dimension—professionals' ways of knowing (Baskett and Marsick, 1992; Wislock and Flannery, 1994)—and an organizational productivity dimension—a comparative perspective and strategic planning (Knox, 1993; Titmus, 1981, 1989).

Considering the continuum of professional education from a broad and integrative perspective can be beneficial in several ways. First, recognizing the characteristics of professional occupations can enable those characteristics to serve as goals of lifelong professional education (Houle, 1980). Second, assistance with the transition from preprofessional education to professional practice can be facilitated (Knox, 1974). For example, there may be benefits to university faculty and CPE providers working with organizations that employ professionals in the early stages of their careers. Third, attention to a learning continuum may facilitate the design of preprofessional education so that it encourages and sustains lifelong professional education (Knox, 1974; Houle, 1980). For example, preprofessional education programs may be able to incorporate both teaching strategies and curriculum design that demonstrate the need for lifelong learning in the professions. Fourth, developing an appreciation of the value of learning communities may assist professionals to seek out practice opportunities where learning communities exist (Palmer, 1998). Fifth, understanding professionals' ways of knowing and perspective transformations (Baskett and Marsick, 1992; Mezirow and Associates, 1990; Mezirow, 1991) as components of the continuum can foster development throughout professional careers. Finally, broadened perspectives on lifelong learning that encompass professional education can facilitate the professional's development in many areas, including family, leisure, and citizen roles (Merriam and Brockett, 1997). This is not meant to be an exhaustive list of the benefits of further development of a continuum of professional practice and education; rather, it is meant to illustrate ways in which attention to the development and expansion of this continuum can benefit both CPE and preprofessional education.

Guidelines for Developing a Continuum of Practice and Education

The perspective provided by a review of these and other writings on the continuum of professional education yields useful and interrelated guidelines for continuing professional education practitioners regarding coordination, responsiveness to learners, encouraging application, and stakeholder support.

Coordination. Coordination of professional education at any stage of the preprofessional–continuing education continuum entails program development decisions by coordinators regarding components such as goals, learning activities, providers, resources, context, and negotiation (see Ottoson, Chapter Five, this volume). Each of these areas is explored briefly here.

Houle (1980) provides a comprehensive rationale for fourteen goals of lifelong professional education on which continuing education programs can focus:

1. Clarifying the defining function of the profession
2. Mastery of theoretical knowledge
3. Capacity to solve problems
4. Use of practical knowledge
5. Self-enhancement beyond professional specialty
6. Formal training
7. Credentialing
8. Creation of a subculture
9. Legal reinforcement
10. Public acceptance
11. Ethical practice
12. Penalties
13. Relations to other vocations
14. Relations to users of service

The relative emphasis on education of each of these goals shifts across the continuum of practice. For instance, use of practical knowledge in preparatory education may include goals for the number of hours learners spend in a clinical setting, whereas in CPE this same goal may mean that the CPE provider finds ways to incorporate practical knowledge within the CPE program itself.

Another component of program development focuses on the learning activities in which participants engage and that educators can facilitate. Houle (1980) notes that more than half of continuing learning in the professions is self-directed, so professional education programs should build on, encourage, and complement self-directed learning. Facilitation of self-directed learning by CPE practitioners includes such activities as clarifying the main purposes of professional education, helping learners set priorities, emphasizing assistance regarding lifelong self-directed education, assisting learners to assess their educational needs, identifying accessible educational resources, helping learners evaluate their self-directed learning efforts, and supporting study of self-directed learning (Knox, 1974). As educators across the continuum encourage self-directed learning, likely benefits include active learning, increased application, and greater demand for challenging professional education.

Providers of professional education include many educational institutions, but also professional associations and enterprises where people work, in which there are increasing opportunities for practica, internships, and preceptorships as part of preprofessional and professional education. As a result, coordination entails strengthening the support received from such organizations. For example, Votruba (1981) urges alignment of continuing education with the main mission of the parent organization (university, employer, and association). This can be accomplished by joint planning, selecting priorities valued by the parent organization, and broadening the base of cooperation. Universities are also broadening their outreach mission to include teaching, research, and service through external partnerships, which can further strengthen the continuum of professional education (Fear and Sandmann, 1995). For example, professional development schools that feature not only internships but also exchanges of faculty and professionals can benefit both university professors and professionals.

Acquisition and allocation of resources can facilitate or hinder cooperation among providers of professional education. Thus, coordination of professional education also includes acquisition of resources such as time, funding, facilities, and various types of cooperation (Green, Grosswald, Suter, and Walthall, 1984). In this exchange, many professional education programs achieve mutually beneficial exchanges with a variety of partners (Queeney, 1997b). For example, collaboration by a law school and bar association can benefit and maximize the resources of each organization.

Coordination of professional education is influenced by the broader societal context of the program's service area (Kegan, 1994). Such societal influences affect the entire continuum of professional education, both directly and indirectly. Direct influences include trends in each professional field that affect supply and demand for people to work in the profession, obsolescence of professional knowledge, and the willingness of people to pay the costs of the education. Indirect influences include competing priorities within the parent organization and competing programs by other providers. Societal threats and opportunities tend to be more difficult to recognize than internal strengths and weaknesses, but they can constitute more powerful influences. For example, current turbulence in the health care field is a major influence on the continuum of professional education. Coordination of professional education should include monitoring of such influences so as to allow strategic positioning of organizations for survival and service (Apps, 1988, 1994; Knox, 1993).

A final generalized aspect of coordination deals with the negotiation of varied expectations regarding goals and activities to achieve those goals. As important as program development and coordination concepts and activities are, coordination of professional education also entails negotiation to win and maintain cooperation among various stakeholders (Knox, 1991; Cervero and Wilson, 1994, 1996). Over the years, much of the initiative to negotiate came from the continuing education side, but as continuing education has moved from the margins of provider organizations toward the core, efforts to collaborate have become more mutual ("Commission to Implement. . .," 1996; Hjorting-Hanson, 1996; Magneson, 1996; Mann, 1994; Palmer and Katsinas, 1996; and Woodsworth and others, 1994).

Responsiveness to Learners. Closely related to coordination is program responsiveness to learners. Preprofessional education programs typically select applicants who meet the admission criteria and quotas, and then address responsiveness in the interests of student achievement. By contrast, continuing professional education programs more often address responsiveness to hard-to-reach members of the profession to encourage them to enroll (Darkenwald and Larson, 1980).

Being responsive and encouraging practitioner growth throughout the continuum of professional education entails attention to both individual and societal aspects. Personal ability and motivation are affected by societal influences such as new knowledge, professional image, relative power, and supply and demand in the profession (Nowlen, 1988). Because, as noted earlier, a majority of continuing learning in the professions is self-directed, a challenge to preprofessional education is to encourage and support self-direction so that more students become lifelong learners (Houle, 1980; Knox, 1974).

Related to responsiveness is empowerment to liberate learners from restricted views of what is possible. Some restrictions are personal, such as stereotypical images of opportunities that may discourage women and minorities from aspiring to professional roles previously held by white males. Some restrictions are societal, in the form of unwritten rules that restrict mobility, such as the glass ceiling in enterprises. Responsiveness to learners helps professionals at all points on the continuum of professional education to make explicit such restrictions and gain greater responsibility and insight to guide their careers (Cervero and Wilson, 1996; Cranton, 1996).

Encouraging Application. A major goal of the entire continuum of professional education is to encourage learners to apply what they learn, with resulting individual and organizational benefits. In preprofessional education this may take the form of practica, preceptorships, internships, and service learning projects. Simulations and supervised practica in actual practice settings help preservice learners relate theory and practice as they seek to solve ill-defined problems (Palmer, 1998; Wislock and Flannery, 1994). In continuing professional education, practitioners are already immersed in professional tasks from which educational needs arise and to which enhanced proficiencies are applied (Nowlen, 1988). The relation between work and education is concurrent and reciprocal. Challenges and changes in the workplace are sources of learning goals and activities, as well as spurs to participation in continuing professional education activities (Willis, Dubin, and Associates, 1990; see also Mott, Chapter Three, and Daley, Chapter Four, this volume).

Familiarity with the continuum of professional education can contribute to strengthening both preprofessional and continuing education. Content and methods from preprofessional education can be used to enrich continuing education. Successful continuing education programs for professionals in the early years of practice can suggest curricular revision for preprofessional education (James of Rusholme, 1972), such as occurred in recent decades as law schools increased their emphasis on lawyering. A reported benefit to professional school faculty members who conduct continuing education activities is the content and methods they discover in continuing education and adapt for use in their preprofessional education teaching. Recent examples have been reported in such fields as medicine (Mann, 1994), dentistry (Hjorting-Hanson, 1996), pharmacy ("Commission to Implement. . .," 1996), social work (Magneson, 1996), librarianship (Woodsworth and others, 1994), and community college administration (Palmer and Katsinas, 1996).

Some activities combine preprofessional and continuing professional education. Examples include educational activities for current practitioners who supervise preprofessional education students in practica in fields such as teaching, social work, nursing, medicine, pharmacy, and engineering. Action learning projects illustrate the value of systemic approaches to team and organization development that are also reflected in quality improvement efforts.

Stakeholder Support. Throughout the continuum of professional education there are multiple stakeholders whose support influences the quality of professional education. Some stakeholders, such as learners, instructors, and administrators, are internal to the program. Others, such as policymakers, supervisors, funders, accreditors, and representatives of collaborative organizations, are largely external to the program. A challenge to leaders of professional education is to obtain support from both sets of stakeholders (Knox, 1982).

Central to such support is provision for each stakeholder to contribute to planning and implementation with tasks and levels of effort that are mutually beneficial. Cervero (1988) indicates distinctive contributions by the major providers, such as educational institutions, associations, enterprises, and consultants. Increasing use of educational technology (in terms of content, methods, instructors, and learner interaction) is affecting both program offerings and stakeholder support across the continuum of professional education (Rossman and Rossman, 1995).

Future Directions

Among the many future directions for professional education that could be explored, two seem especially pertinent to issues on the continuum of learning for the professions: relations among providers and attention to research and evaluation.

Providers. Each of the three main types of providers of professional education (colleges and universities, professional associations, and enterprises) have distinctive resources, assets, and limitations (see Mott, Chapter Three, this volume). Each type of provider has also contributed in distinctive ways to preprofessional and continuing education segments of the continuum (Houle, 1980; Cervero, 1988). For example, preprofessional education by colleges of engineering has emphasized the knowledge base, and in preprofessional education for nurses, hospitals have emphasized clinical practica. Associations have been major providers of continuing legal education directly following law school, and professional associations assume a similarly critical role for physicians following medical school. Cooperation and competition have each been widespread.

However, as Cervero noted in Chapter One of this volume, in recent years there has been increasing collaboration that suggests that various forms of cooperation may become more widespread. Examples include program cosponsorship, production of materials for widespread and integrated use, and train-the-trainer pyramids in which consultants prepare state leaders to conduct educational programs for local practitioners. Another example is interprofessional education such as occurs between physicians and lawyers or physicians and accountants (Hjorting-Hanson, 1996; Queeney, 1997a). Influences on such collaboration include understanding the continuum of professional education, increasing change and knowledge obsolescence, competition among providers, recognition of complimentarity, emphasis on accountability, accreditation, rising costs of education, and educational technology (Apps, 1988; Knox, 1982; Millard, 1991). Each type of provider has distinctive features that can be taken into account in the form of complimentarity, which along with shared goals and benefits is important for successful collaboration. In each provider organization, a major leadership challenge is strengthening internal support for continuing education (Votruba, 1981). One way to do so is to emphasize the continuum of professional education. Foundations can help strengthen the continuum, as illustrated by the recent initiative on preparation for the professions by the Carnegie Foundation for the Advancement of Teaching (see www.carnegiefoundation.org/programinfo.html).

Research. There is research and writing on preprofessional and continuing education generally, and some writing is more focused on specific professional fields. But as noted earlier, there is very little on the continuum of professional education overall. Future research on this topic can build on past work and can set future directions for the field of CPE. Many topics related to program development and leadership for educational programs for adults are also relevant for professional education (Knox, 1991). In a few professional fields, there have been reviews and critiques of the current knowledge base and identification of promising research directions (Davis and Fox, 1994). The main sources of such research have been universities and professional associations (Adelson, Watkins, and Caplan, 1985).

Much of the research on professional education has focused on description, evaluation, and analysis of process and outcomes of current programs. During the 1990s there has been increasing attention to transformation of current perspectives, first from the standpoint of learners and more recently from the perspective of organizations (Cranton, 1996; Mezirow and Associates, 1990; Mezirow, 1991; Schön, 1987). A promising direction regarding evaluation and research is analysis of influences on discrepancies between current and desirable professional education programs (see Ottoson, Chapter Five, this volume). An illustrative research approach would be to have program administrators in both preprofessional and continuing professional education rate Houle's (1980) fourteen goals of professional education relative to both current and desired emphasis. Other promising research directions include self-directed learning, instructional technology, and comparative analysis of professional education across professional fields and national settings.

Conclusion

In conclusion, the continuum of professional education can be strengthened by attention to relations among providers, as well as by research and evaluation. Such efforts can be enhanced by appreciation of a comprehensive and integrated perspective on this continuum, use of insights from relevant literature, recognition of potential benefits, and application of guidelines regarding coordination, responsiveness, application, and stakeholder support.

References

Adelson, R., Watkins, F. S., and Caplan, R. M. *Continuing Education for the Health Professions*. Rockville, Md.: Aspen Systems, 1985.

Apps, J. W. *Higher Education for a Learning Society: Meeting New Demands for Education and Training*. San Francisco: Jossey-Bass, 1988.

Apps, J. W. *Leadership for the Emerging Age*. San Francisco: Jossey-Bass, 1994.

Baskett, H.K.M., and Marsick, V. J. (eds.). *Professionals' Way of Knowing: New Findings on How to Improve Professional Education*. New Directions for Adult and Continuing Education, no. 55. San Francisco: Jossey-Bass, 1992.

Cervero, R. *Effective Continuing Education for Professionals*. San Francisco: Jossey-Bass, 1988.

Cervero, R. M., Azzaretto, J. F., and Associates. *Visions for the Future of Continuing Professional Education*. Athens: Department of Adult Education, University of Georgia, and Georgia Center for Continuing Education, 1990.

Cervero, R. M., and Scanlan, C. L. (eds.). *Problems and Prospects in Continuing Professional Education*. New Directions for Continuing Education, no. 27. San Francisco: Jossey-Bass, 1985.

Cervero, R. M., and Wilson, A. L. *Planning Responsibly for Adult Education*. San Francisco: Jossey-Bass, 1994.

Cervero, R. M., and Wilson, A. L. (eds.). *What Really Matters in Adult Education Program Planning: Lessons in Negotiating Power and Interests*. New Directions for Adult and Continuing Education, no. 69. San Francisco: Jossey-Bass, 1996.

"Commission to Implement Change in Pharmaceutical Education: Maintaining Our Commitment to Change." *American Journal of Pharmaceutical Education,* 1996, *60*(4) 378–384.

Cranton, P. *Professional Development as Transformative Learning: New Perspectives for Teachers of Adults.* San Francisco: Jossey Bass, 1996.

Darkenwald, B., and Larson, A. (eds.). *Reaching Hard-to-Reach Adults.* New Directions for Continuing Education, no. 8. San Francisco: Jossey-Bass, 1980.

Davis, D. D., and Fox, R. D. (eds.). *The Physician as Learner: Linking Research to Practice.* Chicago: American Medical Association, 1994.

Duning, B., Van Kekerix, M., and Zaborowski, L. *Reaching Learners Through Telecommunications.* San Francisco: Jossey-Bass, 1993.

Fear, F. A., and Sandmann, L. "Unpacking the Service Category: Reconceptualizing University Outreach for the Twenty-First Century." *Continuing Higher Education Review,* 1995, *59*(3), 110–122.

Green, J. S., Grosswald, S. J., Suter, E., and Walthall, D.B.V. (eds.). *Continuing Education for the Health Professions.* San Francisco: Jossey-Bass, 1984.

Hjorting-Hanson, E. "The Future Dental Education Process." *Journal of Dental Education,* 1996, *60*(9), 778–782.

Houle, C. O. *The External Degree.* San Francisco: Jossey-Bass, 1973.

Houle, C. O. *Continuing Learning in the Professions.* San Francisco: Jossey-Bass, 1980.

Houle, C. O. *The Literature of Adult Education: A Bibliographic Essay.* San Francisco: Jossey-Bass, 1992.

James of Rusholme, Lord. *Teacher Education and Training.* London: Her Majesty's Stationery Office, 1972.

Kegan, R. *In Over Our Heads.* Cambridge: Harvard University Press, 1994.

Knox, A. B. "Life-Long Self-Directed Education." In R. J. Blakely (ed.), *Fostering the Growing Need to Learn.* Rockville, Md.: Division of Regional Medical Programs, Bureau of Health Resources Development, 1974.

Knox, A. B. "Organizational Dynamics in University Continuing Professional Education." *Adult Education,* 1982, *32*(3), 117–129.

Knox, A. B. "Educational Leadership and Program Administration." In J. Peters and P. Jarvis (eds.), *Adult Education: Evolution and Achievements in a Developing Field of Study.* San Francisco: Jossey-Bass, 1991.

Knox, A. B. *Strengthening Adult and Continuing Education: A Global Perspective on Synergistic Leadership.* San Francisco: Jossey-Bass, 1993.

Magneson, H. "Open Learning/Distance Education: Is This Social Work Education's New Challenge?" *Human Services in the Rural Environment,* 1996, *19*(4), 16–22.

Mann, K. V. "Educating Medical Students: Lessons from Research in Continuing Education." *Academic Medicine,* 1994, *69*(1), 41–47.

Manning, P. R., and DeBakey, L. *Medicine: Preserving the Passion.* New York: Springer-Velag, 1987.

Merriam, S. B., and Brockett, R. G. *The Profession and Practice of Adult Education.* San Francisco: Jossey-Bass, 1997.

Mezirow, J. *Transformative Dimensions of Adult Learning.* San Francisco: Jossey-Bass, 1991.

Mezirow, J., and Associates. *Fostering Critical Reflection in Adulthood: A Guide to Transformative and Emancipatory Learning.* San Francisco: Jossey-Bass, 1990.

Millard, R. M. *Today's Myths and Tomorrow's Realities: Overcoming Obstacles to Academic Leadership in the Twenty-First Century.* San Francisco: Jossey-Bass, 1991.

Nowlen, P. M. *A New Approach to Continuing Education for Business and the Professions.* Old Tappan, N.J.: Macmillan, 1988.

Palmer, J. C., and Katsinas, S. G. (eds.). *Graduate and Professional Education for Community College Leaders: What It Means Today.* New Directions for Community Colleges, no. 95. San Francisco: Jossey-Bass, 1996.

Palmer, P. J. *The Courage to Teach*. San Francisco: Jossey-Bass, 1998.

Queeney, D. S. "Redefining Competency from a Systems Perspective for the Twenty-First Century." *Continuing Higher Education Review*, 1997a, *61*, 3–11.

Queeney, D. S. *Building Partnerships with Professional Associations*. Workforce Development Series. Washington, D.C.: University Continuing Education Association, 1997b.

Rossman, M. H., and Rossman, M. E. (eds.). *Facilitating Distance Education*. New Directions for Adult and Continuing Education, no. 67. San Francisco: Jossey-Bass, 1995.

Schön, D. A. *Educating the Reflective Practitioner*. San Francisco: Jossey-Bass, 1987.

Titmus, C. J. *Strategies for Adult Education: Practices in Western Europe*. Milton Keynes, England: Open University Press, 1981.

Titmus, C. J. (ed.). *Lifelong Education for Adults: An International Handbook*. Elmsford, N.Y.: Pergamon Press, 1989.

Votruba, J. C. (ed.). *Strengthening Internal Support for Continuing Education*. New Directions for Continuing Education, no. 9. San Francisco: Jossey-Bass, 1981.

Willis, S. L., Dubin, S. S., and Associates. *Maintaining Professional Competence: Approaches to Career Enhancement, Vitality, and Success Throughout a Worklife*. San Francisco: Jossey-Bass, 1990.

Wislock, R. P., and Flannery, D. "Appropriate and Inappropriate Uses of Learners' Experiences: An Example." *Journal of Continuing Higher Education*, 1994, *42*(2), 12–15.

Woodsworth, A. and others. *The Future of Education for Librarianship: Looking Forward from the Past*. Washington, D.C.: Council on Library Resources, 1994.

ALAN B. KNOX is professor of continuing education at the University of Wisconsin–Madison.

3

Continuing professional education evolved out of the need for ongoing learning in the professions. This chapter reviews various models of learning and development in practice and examines the role of continuing professional education as a means of developing professional expertise.

The Development of Professional Expertise in the Workplace

Vivian W. Mott

We are a society based on work. Carnevale (1985) maintains that even more than other social structures such as home, education, religion, and even family, an "increasing portion of our identity" (p. 24) and satisfaction are found in our professions. We are also a learning society, with education an increasingly important factor in all other aspects of our lives, especially in the workplace. As Cervero notes in Chapter One of this volume, continuing professional education in the workplace surpasses that of all other providers combined. Consistently through more than two decades of National Center for Educational Statistics surveys, education related to work has been the most frequently cited (National Center for Educational Statistics, 1995). For those employed in many professions, education and training in the workplace take the form of continuing professional education (CPE), the purpose of which is to improve professional competence and practice. According to Houle (1980, p. 77), CPE "implies some form of learning that advances from a previously established level of accomplishment to extend and amplify knowledge, sensitiveness, or skill." Inherent in this purpose and definition, however, are many issues: How did CPE evolve? Whose responsibility is learning in the professions? How do professionals learn? And how is CPE best accomplished? The purpose of this chapter is to respond to these questions.

The Need for Continuing Professional Education

The notion of learning within the context of work is well grounded. Lindeman ([1926] 1961) and Dewey (1938) both argue for the role of experience and practical relevance in learning. Eraut (1994) specifically cites the formation of early "study societies where people doing the same kind of work facing the same problems began to get together for social discourse and the mutual exchange of ideas" (p. 163). In his landmark work, *Continuing Learning in the Professions,* Houle (1980) suggests that although there certainly were professionals in more ancient times, most likely evolving from the priesthood, it was not until the Enlightenment of the eighteenth century that "both theoretical and practical knowledge began to be built into complex systems" (p. 21). Even then, however, professionals still learned largely in isolation, through apprenticeships, or in small groups, because travel and communication were problematic. In the latter part of the nineteenth century, however, continuing education became more systematic, and professional knowledge became more readily accessible through journals, society conferences, and technical support literature provided by equipment and material manufacturers.

There were other reasons for the rise in CPE—reasons associated with professional accountability, the nature of knowledge, and new models of practice. As the number of professions increased and the public's dependence on them rose as well, members within those professions gained inordinate power and influence over people's lives. It may not be coincidence that this growing dependence eventually brought rising public concern over professional inadequacies and demands by the public and legislative bodies for greater accountability. Professional associations responded to these demands with greater emphasis on standards of performance, continuing education, and licensure and certification processes. In every profession, knowledge obsolescence became an issue as new knowledge, models, and theories were promoted, new technologies were advanced, and innovative practice modalities emerged. Throughout these epistemological changes in the professions, there was also growing acceptance of reflective practice as an exemplary model of professional development and learning. Thus, as the importance and numbers of professions escalated, the need for CPE rose as well.

In 1988, Nowlen wrote that continuing education for business and the professions was the fastest growing segment of higher education; that is still true more than a decade later, with more than $5 billion spent annually on a variety of continuing professional education programs, benefitting more than fifty million professionals. According to Nowlen, there are three models of or approaches to CPE, each undergirded by an often tacit and unexamined philosophy about the nature of knowledge and practice and about the very process of professionalization. The *update model* promotes information-intensive, "heavily didactic short courses [with the] central aim of keeping professionals up to date in their practices" (p. 24), removing the gap between what practitioners might know and do in practice and what they are able to do. The update model, however, is grounded in a "centuries-old positivist paradigm in which knowledge is thought to be an external commodity, a paradigm in which most of us are not taught to be creators of knowledge used in practice, but merely consumers" (Mott, 1998, p. 672). As such, the model fails to account for the subjective, social, and negotiated aspects of knowledge in professional practices that are complex, indeterminate, and value-laden; and as a matter of practicality, using the update model alone, practitioners can never actually keep up with the ever-expanding and quickly obsolete knowledge base that is necessary in professional practice.

According to another model, being current in the knowledge of one's profession is insufficient. In the *competence model,* current and relevant knowledge must be combined with other skills (such as critical thinking or interpersonal relationship skills), personal traits and characteristics (such as initiative or a sense of ethics), an individual schema or self-image as a professional, and self-direction or a motive that serves to direct one's actions in practice. The goal of the competence model is to build curricula based on competencies required in specific work settings and enhanced through relevant exercises, role-playing, case studies, and problem solving. An improvement over the update model, the competence model provides a good picture of what good practice is, but not what it is not or might be. Further, with its emphasis on individual competence, the model fails to recognize the much larger and interdependent nature of practice systems that are influenced by various factors (political, social, organizational, for instance) within those systems (Nowlen, 1988).

The *performance model* addresses these shortcomings as well as those of the update model. The performance model is based on three basic precepts of professional practice: first, practicing professionals are individuals, influenced by their environments, self-images, roles, and values; second, professionals practice in complex networks of interdependent systems; and third, complex performance cannot be significantly affected by any single form of intervention. The performance model recognizes these developmental, social, and interdependent considerations and engages professionals in critical "guided self-assessment, a kind of performance triage . . . [which] brings more than job functions into view" (Nowlen, 1988, p. 86). Rather than ask, *What must the professional know?* (as in the update model) or *What must the professional do in a broader sense?* (as in the competence model), the performance model asks, and therefore challenges continuing professional education to answer, What is the professional all about?

Thus, the rise of the professions, societal, epistemological, and technological changes, models or views of developing professional competence, and even practice setting all exert powerful, interactive influences on CPE. Given these divergent influences, another crucial consideration regarding CPE is that of responsibility for the development, implementation, and evaluation of learning in the professions.

Where Does Responsibility for CPE Reside?

Responsibility for providing CPE is assumed by a wide variety of organizations, institutions, and individuals. Although the most commonly thought of are professional associations (the American Medical Association, for instance) and formal educational institutions (colleges, universities, and professional schools), CPE opportunities are also developed and implemented by independent education and training brokers, by manufacturers and suppliers of professional supplies and equipment, and by professionals themselves, either individually or in small groups as well as in employment settings. In fact, according to Houle (1980, p. 167), the "most widely diffused major provider[s] of continuing professional education" are individual practitioners learning either individually or in autonomous groups that vary in size and structure. In many cases, these casually initiated groups frequently evolved into more structured and frequently elitist professional societies.

The tradition of CPE being sponsored by formal educational institutions is a strong if not particularly long-standing convention. With the move toward professionalization, a shift occurred in the arena of preprofessional training, from training professionals within specific practice contexts to colleges and universities. Although more abstract and less contextualized, this more formalized mode of instruction was considered the more legitimate mode; thus the promotion and delivery of CPE within this venue was also perceived as more desirable.

Livneh and Livneh (1999) are among many who have suggested the need for preprofessional training programs to incorporate CPE into the curriculum. In so doing, new professionals not only develop skills of lifelong independent learning, but also begin a habit of engaging in CPE activities as "practitioners who believe in and will continue their professional development" (p. 102). Proponents argued that such integration supports the concept of lifelong professional education and involves important stakeholders, such as employers and professional associations, in the full spectrum of professional knowledge building (Hunt, 1992). In this view of CPE as an extension of one's preparatory education (see Knox, Chapter Two, this volume) throughout the stages of one's professional career, "learning agendas [may be] specifically designed to meet professionals' practice-oriented educational needs" (Stern and Queeney, 1992, p. 16).

Theirs is not a new idea, of course. Houle (1980) argues that CPE is a matter of professional socialization as well as a curricular goal. Houle maintains that "much of every professional's attitude toward future learning and the ability to undertake it has been established by the time of entry into service" (p. 90). Houle warns, in fact, that if the custom of continuing to learn is not established in the years of preservice instruction, the failure to practice it will have increasingly serious consequence. Preservice students do not have time in school to "cover the ground" (p. 85), and later will not know how to do so.

How Professionals Learn

Houle (1980, p. 1) describes professionals as "deeply versed in advanced and subtle bodies of knowledge, which they apply with dedication in solving complex practical problems." Professionals learn, Houle maintains, through "study, apprenticeship, and experience, both by expanding their comprehension of formal disciplines and by finding new ways to use them to achieve specific ends, constantly moving forward and backward from theory to practice so that each enriches the others" (p. 1). Following this broad explanation of how professionals learn in practice, Houle delineated a basic model of the process of professional learning, a process beginning with general education that includes some content specialization, preservice education, certification of competence (after which one is usually inducted into the professional fold), and finally continued education. Houle also suggests that continuing professional education at any level consists of three modes of learning that frequently overlap: instruction, inquiry, and performance. In the *instruction* mode, learning is typically passive and consists of the dissemination of predetermined knowledge and skills. Learning in the *inquiry* mode tends to be exploratory and cooperative, resulting in a synthesis or creation of new techniques or concepts. Learning by *performance* is more active and involves practice in the actual work setting. Although the following models cut across the spectrum of professional learning, all of them emphasize Houle's inquiry and performance modes of learning.

Mental Schema Model. Much of our understanding of how professionals learn in their workplaces is based on cognitive psychology, in which "learning is [seen as] an active, constructive, and goal-oriented process that is dependent upon the mental activities of the learner" (Shuell, 1986, p. 415). According to Shuell, learning occurs when new knowledge is rearranged according to various schema, or easily recognized interpretations or models of interrelated information. One particularly useful schema is that of declarative knowledge, or knowledge about something (such as knowing about a program planning model), and procedural knowledge, or knowledge of how to do something (such as conducting a task analysis as part of planning a program). Ausubel, Novak, and Hanesian's (1978) and Novak's (1998) work on meaningful or relevant learning is also based on a model of cognitive schema, in which new information is associated with other cognitive structures or schemas already present for the learner. According to Ausubel and his colleagues, meaningful learning is more than merely learning meaningful material; it is the acquisition of *new* meaning. Learners engaged in meaningful learning craft their own idiosyncratic significance for new information, making the learning both new and more relevant through its application to a specific context. As such, meaningful learning has significant advantages over rote learning because it is retained longer, facilitates subsequent learning of related information, and is more likely to be transferable to new contexts.

Skill Acquisition Model. In a related model, Dreyfus and Dreyfus (1986) propose that practitioners learn in the context of practice and develop their skills according to a progression from novice to advanced beginner, to competent, to proficient, and finally to expert. In the Dreyfus model of skill acquisition, the emphasis is on learning from experience, utilizing increasing perception and intuitive recognition of systems within practical situations, rather than action based on rote learning. As practitioners progress through the stages of skill acquisition, there is a decrease in rule-guided behavior in lieu of more holistic *knowing how.* (See Daley, Chapter Four, this volume, for an expanded discussion of this model.)

In support of the skill acquisition model, convention suggests that practitioners learn in one setting (university classroom or laboratory) and then transfer that knowledge as needed to the practice setting. Such knowledge is initially objectified and instrumental, drawn as it is from outside the learner. More current thought, however, proposes that practitioners actually create new knowledge out of the experiences and context of their work environment (Daley, 1998; Mott, 1996, 1998). While novice practitioners depend on and learn from concepts gained from external authorities, more experienced practitioners tend to learn through self-initiated, action-oriented, informal mechanisms, constructing "a knowledge base for themselves in the context of their practice" (Daley, 1998, p. 429). According to Daley, this constructivist learning process changes the "character and meaning of both the new information and the previous experience, . . . [resulting in] a deeper level of meaning and understanding in the process" (p. 431).

Schön's Reflective Practitioner Model. Much of the learning that takes place in one's profession comes about in response to the problems of the practice itself. As Schön (1983) notes, the high, hard ground of preprofessional education and training on which the techniques and theories are learned soon gives way to the swamp in which practice actually occurs. In his critique of "technical rationality . . . [which] fails to account for practical competence in 'divergent' situations" (p. 49), Schön cites the limitations of the positivist approach to solving the problems of the complexities of the modern world. A reflective practice model, Schön argues, better explains the "epistemology of practice implicit in the artistic, intuitive processes that some practitioners bring to situations of uncertainty, instability, uniqueness, and value conflict" (p. 49).

Reflection, according to Schön, is a social process embedded in practice. Schön suggests that practitioners increasingly find themselves in ambiguous, ill-defined, and conflicting situations for which the theories and models they learned do not prepare them. Instead, Schön argues, practitioners rely on practical experience, tacit and intuitive knowledge, and reflection-in-action to solve the problems of professional practice. He maintains that our knowing is *in* the actions of our practice, and he explains that "reflection tends to focus interactively on the outcomes of action, the action itself, and the intuitive knowing implicit in the action" (1983, p. 56). Schön suggests that learning reflection-in-action is a developmental process in which practitioners first learn a system of rules and procedures, recognize their appropriate application within particular situations, and then develop and verify new forms of knowing in actual practice situations.

Other Models of Learning in Practice. There are numerous other discussions of learning in practice and the development of professional expertise, some of them adaptations of the preceding models and holding promise for further thinking about learning in the context of work. According to

Mott (1996, p. 62), for example, "expert knowledge [is best] generated by those . . . who have a vested interest" in the dynamics of professional practice. Practitioners create expert knowledge for use in practice through a process she terms *reflective theory building,* in which the practitioner "consciously reflects on the challenges of practice, reiteratively engages in problem posing, data gathering, action, evaluation, and reflection, and then shares the knowledge produced with others in practice" (p. 61).

Eraut (1994, p. 20) suggests that it is "inappropriate to think of knowledge as first being learned then later being used," because any knowledge applied situationally is no longer the same as when it was learned. Although professionals routinely learn on the job, according to Eraut such learning rarely contributes to general professional knowledge unless time is designated to reflect on the significance or relevance of the situation. Specifically, Eraut suggests that learning within one's profession must include "(1) an appropriate combination of learning settings . . ., (2) time for study, consultation and reflection, (3) the availability of suitable learning resources, (4) people who are prepared (i.e., both willing and able) to give appropriate support and (5) the learner's own capacity to learn and take advantage of the opportunities available" (p. 13).

Toward a New Model of Developing Professional Expertise

Professionals then develop and use increasingly complex systems of thinking, continually adding to their already rich repertoire of practical knowledge. Schön (1983, 1987), Cervero (1988, 1992a, 1992b), and others have maintained that the knowledge actually used in day-to-day practice—the routine as well as the complex and conflicting—is the knowledge learned in practice, and that the challenges and complexities of practice itself, and reflection on these challenges and complexities, are the richest source of learning for the professional. According to Cervero (1992a, p. 91), the "popular wisdom among practising professionals is that the knowledge they acquire from practice is far more useful than what they acquire from the more formal forms of education." This situated knowledge, created out of the tools, contexts, and experiences of professional practice and learned through feedback from the practice environment, is "made meaningful by the context by which it is acquired" (p. 95).

Cervero (1988, 1990, 1992b) suggests that perhaps a valuable model for developing professional expertise might be based in learning from and within practice. Without maintaining that professionals can do without the abstract knowledge learned in most of preprofessional and much of continuing professional education, Cervero suggests, instead, that CPE promotes two other forms of knowing for use in practice. In addition to formal theory or technical *knowledge that,* practitioners should also employ both practical knowledge and the "process by which professionals use their practical knowledge to construct an understanding of current situations of practice" (1988, p. 55). Practical knowledge, or what cognitive psychologists call procedural knowledge or *knowledge how,* includes examples, metaphors, case studies, stories, and scenarios derived from practice itself. The processes by which practitioners further construct understanding may include reflection-in-action (Schön, 1987), reflective theory building (Mott, 1996), constructivist knowing (Daley, 1998), and problem posing (Ausubel, Novak, and Hanesian, 1978). Thus, Cervero (1988) and others have suggested that one of the more effective means of fostering these two forms of knowing in practice is by encouraging professionals to "become researchers of their own practice" (p. 56).

Conclusion

A few common themes run throughout all of these models. In keeping with the tenets of the models described in this chapter, effective CPE with the goal of developing professional expertise should be

- Dynamic and reflective of the changing environments present in most professional practice
- Authentic, with an emphasis on relevant formative and summative self-assessment
- Practice-based, that is, situated in and drawn from the complexities of practice itself
- Collaborative, with a focus on communities of practice rather than on individual practitioners
- Future oriented, ensuring effective practice and competence for tomorrow as well as today

If the goal of CPE is development of professional expertise for the improvement of practice, the most effective means are practitioners' dialogue, reflection-in-action, and theory building, in which knowledge is generated from "new examples, understandings, and actions . . . [and added to] already existing repertoires" (Cervero, 1988, p. 158). Formal continuing education and training are of course also important, and their initial benefit is heightened by practitioners' engagement in actual practice situations. CPE programs that are dynamic, authentic, practice based, collaborative, and future oriented offer practitioners a broadened concept of professional development in keeping with the performance model. Such a model of CPE, of learning from and within practice, would help ensure more effective career practitioners and improved professional practice for society.

References

Ausubel, D. P., Novak, J. D., and Hanesian, H. *Educational Psychology: A Cognitive View.* (2nd ed.) Austin, Tex.: Holt, Rinehart and Winston, 1978.

Carnevale, A. P. *Jobs for the Nation: Challenges for a Society Based on Work.* Alexandria, Va.: American Society for Training and Development, 1985.

Cervero, R. M. *Effective Continuing Education for Professionals*. San Francisco: Jossey-Bass, 1988.

Cervero, R. M., Azzaretto, J. J., and Associates. (Eds.). *Visions for the Future of Continuing Professional Education*. Athens: University of Georgia Continuing Education Center, 1990.

Cervero, R. M. "Professional Practice, Learning, and Continuing Education: An Integrated Perspective." *International Journal of Lifelong Education*, 1992a, *11*(2), 91–101.

Cervero, R. M. "Cooperation and Collaboration in the Field of Continuing Professional Education. In E. S. Hunt (ed.), *Professional Workers as Learners*. Washington, D.C.: Office of Educational Research and Improvement, U.S. Department of Education, 1992b.

Daley, B. J. "Novice and Expert Learning: Impact on Training." Proceedings of the Academy of Human Resource Development (pp. 427–433), Washington, D.C., Mar. 5–8, 1998.

Dewey, J. *Experience and Education*. New York: Collier Books, 1938.

Dreyfus, H. L., and Dreyfus, S. E. *Mind over Machine: The Power of Human Intuition and Expertise in the Era of the Computer*. Oxford, U.K.: Basil Blackwell, 1986.

Eraut, M. *Developing Professional Knowledge and Competence*. Washington, D.C.: Falmer Press, 1994.

Houle, C. O. *Continuing Learning in the Professions*. San Francisco: Jossey-Bass, 1980.

Hunt, E. S. (ed.). *Professional Workers as Learners: The Scope, Problems, and Accountability of Continuing Professional Education in the 1990s*. Washington, D.C.: Office of Educational Research and Improvement, U.S. Department of Education, 1992.

Lindeman, E. C. *The Meaning of Adult Education*. Norman: University of Oklahoma, 1961. (Originally published 1926.)

Livneh, S., and Livneh, H. "Continuing Professional Education Among Educators: Predictors of Participation in Learning Activities." *Adult Education Quarterly*, 1999, *49*(2), 91–106.

Mott, V. W. "Knowledge Comes from Practice: Reflective Theory Building in Practice." In R. W. Rowden (ed.), *Workplace Learning: Debating Five Critical Questions of Theory and Practice*. New Directions for Adult and Continuing Education, no. 72. San Francisco: Jossey-Bass, 1996.

Mott, V. W. "Professionalization and Reflective Theory Building in HRD." Proceedings of the Academy of Human Resource Development (pp. 671–676), Washington, D.C., Mar. 5–8, 1998.

National Center for Educational Statistics. *Statistics in Brief: Forty Percent of Adults Participate in Adult Education Activities: 1994–1995*. (NCES 95–823) Washington, D.C.: U.S. Department of Education, Office of Educational Research and Improvement, 1995.

Nowlen, P. M. *A New Approach to Continuing Education for Business and the Professions*. Old Tappan, N.J.: Macmillan, 1988.

Novak, J. D. *Learning, Creating, and Using Knowledge*. Hillsdale, N.J.: Erlbaum, 1998.

Schön, D. A. *The Reflective Practitioner*. New York: Basic Books, 1983.

Schön, D. A. *Educating the Reflective Practitioner*. San Francisco: Jossey-Bass, 1987.

Shuell, T. J. "Cognitive Conceptions of Learning." *Review of Educational Research*, 1986, *56*, 411–436.

Stern, M. R., and Queeney, D. S. "The Scope of Continuing Professional Education: Providers, Consumer, Issues." In E. S. Hunt (ed.), *Professional Workers as Learners: The Scope, Problems, and Accountability of Continuing Professional Education in the 1990s*. Washington, D.C.: Office of Educational Research and Improvement, U.S. Department of Education, 1992.

VIVIAN W. MOTT is assistant professor in the Department of Counselor and Adult Education, East Carolina University, Greenville, North Carolina.

4

This chapter explores how professionals construct knowledge in the context of their practice by connecting concepts from their experiences and continuing professional education activities.

Learning in Professional Practice

Barbara J. Daley

Learning within continuing professional education (CPE) programs is a central issue for practice development. As providers of CPE we often assume that attendance at our programs constitutes learning for professionals and that they will automatically use the information they receive when they return to their work sites.

But what do we, as CPE providers, really know about how participants learn to use new information? We know that many professionals attend CPE only to shelve the large handouts and course materials they receive, never to look at them again (Nowlen, 1988). We know that the theory or new knowledge taught in CPE programs is seldom transferred immediately and directly to the practice arena (Ottoson, 1995). We know that most CPE programs are more effective in teaching novices than in fostering the professional development of experts (Daley, 1999; Desforges, 1995). Finally, we know there are factors in the work environment that inhibit practitioners from incorporating what they have learned in a CPE program into their practice (Daley, 1997; Eraut, 1994).

Despite the issues identified in the preceding paragraph, we also know that practitioners do use information from CPE programs in their practice, often in ways that are totally unintended by program planners (Daley, 1997). We know that it is extremely difficult to evaluate the outcomes of CPE programs because use of the program's material is often idiosyncratic to the learner (see Ottoson, Chapter Five, this volume).

To be truly effective in CPE, we must include a model of learning (Cervero, 1988) at the heart of our education practice. As Eraut (1994) explains, behind "professional education lies a remarkable ignorance about professional learning" (p. 40). Previous models of learning have relied on ideas about technical rationality (Houle, 1980), transfer of learning (Broad and Newstrom, 1992) and adoption of innovation (Rogers, 1995). In these views, knowledge for professional practice was created in one location, often a university setting; disseminated through CPE programs; and then transferred to or adopted in professional practice. Using these models of learning, educators tended to create educational programs that provided up-date information rather than fostering a continuum of professional practice development (see Knox, Chapter Two, this volume).

In this chapter, I advocate reframing CPE to include a constructivist view of learning created by linking professional practice, context, and knowledge in an integrated learning system. This chapter expands the notions of transfer of learning and adoption of innovation, proposing a perspective of learning from which continuing professional education can be reframed.

Previous Learning Model in Continuing Professional Education

Cervero (1988) proposes a model for learning in the professions that is based on an understanding of how professionals "develop knowledge through practice" (p. 39). He incorporates cognitive psychology, reflective practice (Schön, 1987), and studies of expertise (Benner, 1984; Dreyfus and Dreyfus, 1985) into this model. Cervero advocates that CPE providers should develop a critical model of the learner that integrates the development of two forms of knowledge—technical and practical. Both forms are necessary to incorporate scientific principles into cases, examples, and real-life experiences.

Cervero's model of the learner has expanded our understanding of the multiple forms of knowledge needed in professional practice. It is now time to enlarge this model, to integrate both professional practice and context into our construct of professional learning.

Expanded Model of Learning in Continuing Professional Education

Recent research indicates that professionals construct a knowledge base for themselves in the context of their practice by linking concepts from new knowledge with their practice experiences. At this point, they actively make decisions on how to incorporate new knowledge into the context of practice based on their interpretations of the environment. In a previous study (Daley, 1997) in which professionals were interviewed about how they learned, I asked a nurse how she made connections between the client care she provided and knowledge from CPE programs. She told me, "Well, I don't think of it like that, I mean I can't really say what helps me deal with what. I think of it more like creating mosaics. I mean, you have all these little pieces that come from all over and in and of themselves they don't mean much, but when you put them together you have a beautiful picture. Continuing education and client care are more like that for me. I take little pieces of what I learn from many places and put them together until I have my own picture" (p. 109).

This metaphor of "creating mosaics" depicts the process of actively constructing a knowledge base from practice. In expanding Cervero's model of the learner, we need to further develop an understanding of how knowledge is constructed, how it is linked with professional practice, and how the context affects the process (see Figure 4.1).

Knowledge Construction for Professional Practice. In the model of learning depicted in Figure 4.1, knowledge is viewed as a social construction of information that occurs through a process of constructivist and transformative learning. Combining these two perspectives allows us to understand how the learner creates a knowledge base yet changes it when faced with practice experiences. Context and professional practice are then linked to knowledge development to complete the learning model depicted.

Constructivist Learning Theory. Constructivists believe that individuals create knowledge by linking new information with past experiences (Bruner, 1990; Novak, 1998; Novak and Gowin, 1984). Within a constructivist framework, the learner progressively differentiates concepts into more and more complex understandings and also reconciles abstract understanding with concepts garnered from previous experience. Learners make knowledge meaningful by the ways in which they establish connections among

Figure 4.1. Model of Learning in CPE

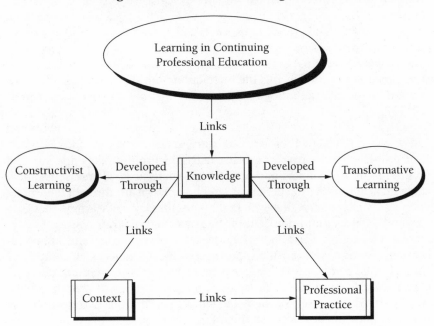

knowledge learned, previous experiences, and the context in which they find themselves.

Lambert and others (1995, pp. 17–18) identify multiple principles of constructivist learning theory. They indicate that knowledge and beliefs must be formed within the learner, so that the learner can give their experiences meaning. Additionally, they contend that learning is a social activity; thus learning activities should foster learner access to their own unique experiences. Finally, they emphasize reflection and metacognition as essential components of knowledge construction.

In summary, constructivists believe that learning is a process of probing deeply the meaning of experiences in our lives, and developing an understanding of how these experiences shape understanding. Within a constructivist framework, learning activities are designed to foster an integration of thinking, feeling, and acting while helping participants learn how to learn (Novak and Gowin, 1984).

Learning in the context of professional practice is also informed by the growing body of work in the area of situated cognition (Brown, Collins, and Dugid, 1989; Lave and Wenger, 1991; Wilson, 1993). Situated cognition can be conceptualized as having four interrelated learning aspects: (1) learning that is situated in the context of authentic practice, (2) transfer limited to similar situations, (3) learning as a social phenomenon, and (4) learning that relies on use of prior knowledge (Black and Schell, 1995). In this view, the authentic "activity in which knowledge is developed and deployed . . . is not separable from, or ancillary to, learning and cognition. Nor is it neutral. Rather, it is an integral part of what is learned" (Brown, Collins, and Duguid, 1989, p. 32). According to Wilson (1993), "Learning is thus an everyday event that is social in nature because it occurs with other people; it is 'tool dependent' because the setting provides mechanisms (computers, maps, measuring cups) that aid and, more important, structure the cognitive process; and, finally, it is the interaction with the setting itself in relation to its social and tool-dependent nature that determines the learning" (p. 73).

Lave and Wenger (1991) have indicated that authentic activity and tools within the context of use help foster the construction of knowledge.

Transformative Learning. Constructivist learning theory and situated cognition help us understand how professionals acquire knowledge, how they make use of their experiences, and how they learn through their practice. In my experience, however, there is another level of learning that goes beyond what we can understand from constructivist frameworks. Professionals will often describe how they learned topics in formal education programs only to have their ideas on those topics change in the context of practice. An emotional encounter with a client or a disorienting dilemma (Mezirow, 1991) in practice may be as important in transforming professionals' perspectives as knowledge acquired in CPE courses. Transformative learning adds to our understanding of these changes.

Transformative learning (Mezirow, 1991, 1997a, 1997b) expands our understanding of constructing knowledge by defining learning as a critically reflective process wherein the learner ultimately assesses previous understandings to determine whether those assumptions still hold in the learner's present situation. Adults learn within this framework by adding to or transforming old meaning schemes, acquiring new meaning schemes, or transforming perspectives.

According to Mezirow (1997a), "a significant personal transformation involving subjective reframing, that is, transforming one's own frame of reference, often occurs in response to a disorienting dilemma through a three-part process: critical reflection on one's own assumptions, discourse to validate the critically reflective insight, and action" (p. 60).

An expanded model of learning in professional practice needs to link the theoretical perspectives of transformative and constructivist learning. Linking these two perspectives provides an explanation of how professionals initially acquire information and then change their understanding of that information based on experience. For example, in recent interviews a nurse shared with me that she saw herself as a relatively good communicator. She had learned communication theory in her basic preparatory program and practiced the skill with her clients while doing assessments and providing treatments. When she worked with a client who was dying, however, this client taught her what it meant to communicate. Her understanding of communication shifted from saying the right thing to being available on the client's terms. "My assumption," she stated, "was that if I said the right words, I was communicating well. After this experience I recognized that I was basing my actions on a view of communication that was not really accurate in my practice. I now believe that communication is about presence, caring, and time, not just words." In this example, the professional learned by constructing an understanding of the concept of communication and by changing her perspective about what communication meant following a significant practice experience.

In another example, a social worker described how her understanding of resistance in working with involuntary clients changed her views on the connections between social work and politics. She indicated that her basic education "labeled people as resistant." She explained the impact of her practice on this perspective: "I learned that when somebody comes to you with a problem, you don't have to spend as much time fixing that person as you do fixing the things around them in the environment. If you listen, you know it is not so much resistance but it's racism, it's poverty. I learned to reconceptualize resistance and focus not so much on the individual in a therapeutic sense but to focus on the system, and to be an advocate at the system level." This social worker indicated that she had constructed a new meaning of the concept of resistance through her practice and that she had transformed her perspective so that her interventions with clients were on a much broader level.

Linking Knowledge and Context. In the expanded model of learning presented in Figure 4.1, context refers to the place where professionals provide care or deliver services to clients. The relationship of context to practice is particularly important because in today's environment professionals are considered organizational employees rather than free, autonomous decision makers (Wilson, Chapter Three, this volume). Grzyb, Graham, and Donaldson (1997) point out that these changing conditions necessitate a deeper understanding of organizational professions, of the impact of bureaucracy on those professions, and of changing organizational dynamics on professional work.

In the model of learning presented here, Bolman and Deal's (1997) framework is added as a way to clarify the connections between knowledge and context. Bolman and Deal demonstrate that organizations can be viewed through four different frames—structural, human resources, political, and symbolic. By viewing a model of learning through these imaginary frames, CPE providers can begin to understand the impact that context has on knowledge construction.

The *structural frame* uses sociological concepts and emphasizes formal roles, defined relationships, and structures that fit the organizational environment and technology. The *human resources frame* posits that organizations consist of individuals with needs and feelings that must be taken into account so that the individuals can learn, grow, and change. The *political frame* analyzes conflict as part of organizational processes. Within this view, the organization is composed of separate groups competing for power and resources. The *symbolic frame* sees organizations as tribes with cultures propelled by rituals, ceremonies, stories, heroes, and myths (Bolman and Deal, 1997).

In professional practice, the context shapes how professionals look at new information, influencing not only what information professionals seek to learn but also what information they try to incorporate into their professional practice. In recent studies (Daley and Carlsson, 1999), my colleague and I found that Bolman and Deal's organizational frames affect the knowledge use of nurses, social workers, and lawyers in ways unique to each profession. For instance, nurses would use the political frame to construct knowledge differently than lawyers or social workers would. Nurses literally screen out information from their practice based on the perception of the political frame. When asked how organizational politics affect their use of knowledge, nurses said, "Well, if I don't have the power to use the information, I just don't even share it." However, social workers responding to the same question indicated, "Well, just because the door is closed does not mean it is locked. There is always a way around that." Social workers indicate that they view dealing with the political context as an integral part of their advocacy role. Lawyers, however, seem to view their work as one-on-one with a client. If they choose to use new information in their practice, they do so regardless of the political system.

Thus, nurses often let the political system block their use of information, social workers recognize the political issues and find creative ways to go around them, and lawyers seldom consider the political issues as having any impact on their use of knowledge. The important point here is that the context affects each of these professions in a manner that is unique to that profession, offering the CPE provider important information for program planning and evaluation.

Developing Professional Practice. Within the CPE literature, two schools of thought exist as to how professionals develop within their practice arenas. One perspective describes professional development as simply the enhancement of thought and information processing skills; the second perspective views professional development as the enhancement of expertise through an artistic-intuitive approach. Both of these views are included in the model of learning described in Figure 4.1.

In the first view, professional development is described as a rational process of information processing, problem solving, decision making, and clinical reasoning and judgment (Bagely-Thompson, 1990; Fonteyn, 1991). Studies with lawyers (Daley and Carlsson, 1999), for instance, indicate that as their practice develops they learn to sort through extraneous issues and get to the heart of the matter quickly and efficiently. Lawyers claim they seldom use an intuitive thought process; rather, they use a highly analytical process that narrows and reduces information to its most elemental form. For instance, one lawyer stated, "The main thing I have to do in my practice is sort through all the information the client presents and get to the bottom line issue to analyze how the issue fits with the law." Lawyers indicate that as they develop their practice, their thinking skills become more and more analytical.

Alternatively, the literature presents a second view of professional development that is described as attaining expertise by taking a more intuitive approach to the topic (Benner, 1984; Dreyfus and Dreyfus, 1985; Eraut, 1994; Schön, 1987). This view of professional development encompasses the ideas of artistry, reflection, and alternative ways of knowing in professional development. Benner (1984) expands our understanding of the development of professional practice by identifying domains of practice on a continuum from novice to expert. This continuum, based on the Dreyfus Model of Skill Acquisition (Dreyfus and Dreyfus, 1985), suggests that professionals develop from novice to expert as they learn to rely on past concrete experiences rather than on abstract principles, as they understand situations as integrated wholes rather than as discrete parts, and as they begin to act as involved performers rather than as detached observers.

One of the most interesting findings in studies comparing novice and expert nurses (Daley, 1999) was that experts have developed an understanding of their own learning processes. Expert nurses, for instance, have learned how to learn in the context of their practice. They know how to search out information and make connections between the new information and their experience. Furthermore, they are willing to change their practice based on the new knowledge they create. Novice nurses, conversely, tend to use learning strategies that are more contingent on others and on the written rules.

In the preceding sections of this chapter, a model for understanding the learning that takes place in CPE (Figure 4.1) has been proposed based on combining literature, research, and experience in the areas of constructivist learning, transformative learning, organizational context, information processing, and professional practice development. This model offers a way by which CPE providers can integrate learning, professional development, and context within their educational activities.

Implications for the Provision of Continuing Professional Education: Creating New Systems of Learning

The model described in this chapter has a number of implications for CPE practice. Obviously this is not an all-inclusive model of learning and it is embedded in assumptions about the nature of knowledge in professional practice and about the contexts of knowledge use.

I believe that enhancing professional practice development requires a new model of learning that incorporates the professional, the work environment, and the practice itself into educational endeavors. Yet basing one's CPE practice on a model of learning or a learning system is a significant change in mind-set for the majority of CPE providers, because this shifts the role from developer of specific program content to facilitator of learning, growth, and change in professional practice. It means that when we as CPE providers create programs, we need to plan actively and incorporate methods that encourage participants to link the content of the program to their actual practice and their work environments. We need to work with participants to help them develop learning strategies and tools that foster a constructivist-transformative approach to practice development. We have been teaching on the assumption that professionals merely transfer information to their practice; instead we should be actively working with them to foster the development and use of educational tools that facilitate knowledge construction in the context of practice. This active facilitation of knowledge construction then enhances the meaning that the professional derives from attendance at a CPE program.

But how can we do this? There are already many educational tools that foster both a constructivist and a transformative view of learning. Consider such tools as concept maps (Novak, 1998), reflective journals, (Brookfield, 1995), vee diagrams, (Novak, 1998), analysis of practice exemplars, (Benner, 1984), critical incidents (Brookfield, 1995), action learning (Brooks and Watkins, 1994), and creating professional learning communities (Eraut, 1994). All can be used to foster a constructivist, transformative, context-based professional practice development program. What these tools have in common is that they create a record of professional practice events or experiences and then allow the professional to reflect on them and make connections between them and the context of their practice. The beauty of these tools is that most often the focus is on linking new knowledge to previous experiences, contexts, and practice.

The key, I believe, is to change our mind-set as CPE providers and to open our program planning and evaluation to new ideas and different ways to incorporate a view of the learner into our CPE practice. Our main challenge as CPE providers is to understand that transfer of learning and adoption of innovation are part of the knowledge construction process and an integral part of professional learning. Thus, when we view professional learning as constructivist and transformative, when we link both context and professional practice to learning, we have then situated and integrated a holistic rather than a segmented and partitioned view of knowledge development.

References

Bagely-Thompson, C., Ryan, S., and Kitzman, H. "Expertise: The Basis for Expert System Development." *Advances in Nursing,* 1990, *13*(1), 3–10.

Benner, P. *From Novice to Expert: Excellence and Power in Clinical Nursing Practice.* Menlo Park, Calif.: Addison-Wesley, 1984.

Black, R., and Schell, J. "Learning Within a Situated Cognition Framework: Implications for Adult Learning." Paper presented at the American Vocational Association Convention, Denver, Colo., 1995. (ED 389 939)

Bolman, L., and Deal, T. *Reframing Organizations: Artistry, Choice, and Leadership.* San Francisco: Jossey-Bass, 1997.

Broad, M. L., and Newstrom, J. W. *Transfer of Training.* Reading, Mass.: Addison-Wesley, 1992.

Brookfield, S. *Becoming a Critically Reflective Teacher.* San Francisco: Jossey-Bass, 1995.

Brooks, A., and Watkins, K. (eds.). *The Emerging Power of Action Inquiry Technologies.* New Directions in Adult and Continuing Education, no. 63. San Francisco: Jossey-Bass, 1994.

Brown, J. S., Collins, A., and Duguid, P. "Situated Cognition and the Culture of Learning." *Educational Researcher,* 1989, *18*(1), pp. 32–43.

Bruner, J. *Acts of Meaning.* Cambridge, Mass.: Harvard University Press, 1990.

Cervero, R. *Effective Continuing Education for Professionals.* San Francisco: Jossey-Bass, 1988.

Daley, B. "Creating Mosaics: The Interrelationships of Knowledge and Context." *Journal of Continuing Education in Nursing,* 1997, *28*(3), 102–114.

Daley, B. "Novice to Expert: An Exploration of How Professionals Learn." *Adult Education* Quarterly, 1999, *49*(4), 133–147.

Daley, B., and Carlsson, M. "Learning in Context: Connections in Continuing Professional Education." Midwest Research to Practice Conference Proceedings, University of Missouri–St. Louis, St. Louis, Sept. 22–24, 1999.

Desforges, C. "How Does Experience Affect Theoretical Knowledge for Teaching?" *Learning and Instruction,* 1995, *5*, 385–400.

Dreyfus, H., and Dreyfus, S. *Mind over Machine: The Power of Human Intuition and Expertise in the Era of the Computer.* New York: Free Press, 1985.

Eraut, M. *Developing Professional Knowledge and Competence.* Washington, D.C.: Falmer Press, 1994.

Fonteyn, M. "Research Review and Implications for Practice: Implications of Clinical Reasoning Studies for Critical Care Nursing." *Focus on Critical Care,* 1991, *18*(4), 322–327.

Grzyb, S., Graham, S. W., and Donaldson, J. F. "Effects of Organizational Role and Culture on Participation in Continuing Professional Education." Paper presented at the Annual Meeting of the American Educational Research Association, Chicago, Mar. 24–28, 1997. (ED 409 284)

Houle, C. O. *Continuing Learning in the Professions.* San Francisco: Jossey Bass, 1980.

Lambert, L., Walker, D., Zimmerman, D. P., Cooper, J. E., Lambert, M. D., Gardner, M. E., and Ford Slack, P. J. *The Constructivist Leader.* New York: Teachers College Press, 1995.

Lave, J., and Wenger, E. *Situated Learning: Legitimate Peripheral Participation.* Cambridge, Mass.: Cambridge University Press, 1991.

Mezirow, J. *Transformative Dimensions of Adult Learning.* San Francisco: Jossey-Bass, 1991.

Mezirow, J. "Transformation Theory Out of Context." *Adult Education Quarterly,* 1997a, *48*(1), 60–62.

Mezirow, J. "Transformative Learning: Theory to Practice." In P. Cranton (ed.), *Transformative Learning in Action: Insights from Practice.* New Directions for Adult and Continuing Education, no. 74. San Francisco: Jossey-Bass, 1997b.

Nowlen, P. *A New Approach to Continuing Education for Business and the Professions: The Performance Model.* Old Tappan, N.J.: Macmillian, 1988.

Novak, J. *Learning, Creating and Using Knowledge: Concept Maps™ as Facilitative Tools in Schools and Corporations.* Hillsdale, N.J.: Erlbaum, 1998.

Novak, J., and Gowin, B. *Learning How to Learn.* Cambridge, Mass.: Cambridge University Press, 1984.

Ottoson, J. "Use of a Conceptual Framework to Explore the Multiple Influences of Application of Learning Following a Continuing Education Program." *Canadian Journal for the Study of Adult Education,* 1995, *9*(2), 1–17.

Rogers, E. M. *Diffusion of Innovations.* New York: Free Press, 1995.

Schön, D. A. *Educating the Reflective Practitioner: Toward a New Design for Teaching and Learning in the Professions.* San Francisco: Jossey-Bass, 1987.

Wilson, A. "The Promise of Situated Cognition." In S. B. Merriam (ed.), *An Update of Adult Learning Theory.* New Directions for Adult and Continuing Education, no. 57. San Francisco: Jossey-Bass, 1993.

BARBARA J. DALEY *is assistant professor of adult and continuing education in the Department of Administrative Leadership at the University of Wisconsin-Milwaukee.*

5

Program evaluation theory seeks to make the evaluation of continuing professional education a transparent process. This chapter introduces the Situated Evaluation Framework, which situates the learner and knowledge assessment at the junction of the educational context, the practice context, and the evaluation context.

Evaluation of Continuing Professional Education: Toward a Theory of Our Own

Judith M. Ottoson

There is nothing so practical as a good theory.
—Lewin (1951, p. 169)

Objectives dominate the focus of evaluation in continuing professional education (CPE). They are clear statements of what will happen to whom or what, by when, and under what circumstances as a result of a program (Mager, 1975). Programs are considered successful if objectives are achieved. Syntheses of the CPE literature suggest that objectives have helped identify CPE effects and establish general causal links between CPE programs and outcomes (Davis, Thomson, Oxman, and Haynes, 1995; Umble and Cervero, 1996; Waddell, 1991). Although objectives prove to be necessary components of CPE evaluation, they are not without problems. Clear objectives can be written for ill-conceived programs. Conditions of performance in classrooms and in the practice context may be unrecognizably different. Objectives as statements of intended CPE outcomes can become confused with thinking about objectives as value-neutral or objective statements. Intended objectives are not the only outcomes of CPE. Evaluation of CPE requires more than good objectives to be effective.

One way to strengthen objective-based evaluation in CPE is to complement it with theory-based evaluation. Such evaluations seek to make transparent intended linkages among program components and outcomes. If Lewin (1951) is right, effective theory-based evaluation can have practical use in the identification of not only feasible outcomes but also the causal moderators that the second wave of CPE evaluation seeks to explain (Umble and Cervero, 1996).

Despite the trend toward theory-based evaluations in the program evaluation field, little evidence of similar effort is found in CPE evaluations. Most of the effort to date in developing a theory of evaluation has been done with broad-scale social programs that are different in scope, duration, and context than CPE programs (Shadish, Cook, and Leviton, 1991). This chapter explores how new directions in program evaluation can enhance evaluation of continuing professional education. The components of evaluation theory are introduced, discussed in relation to their practical application in the CPE context, and applied to an evaluation framework situated in the CPE context.

Components of Effective CPE Evaluation Theory

Theories are statements about how things connect. They may be informal or grand, loosely or tightly constructed, focused on the individual or the collective, and they may extend from the concrete to the abstract. Whatever their form, theories intend to explain why relationships work the way they do (LeCompte and Preissle, 1993; Smith, 1989). Learning theories help explain how adults learn and thereby inform the planning and pedagogy of CPE programs. If learning theories shape CPE planning, what theories shape CPE evaluation?

"The fundamental purpose of program evaluation theory is to specify feasible practices that evaluators can use to construct knowledge of the value of social programs that can be used to ameliorate the social problems to which programs are relevant" (Shadish, Cook, and Leviton, 1991, p. 36). Tucked into this wordy purpose are the components of *effective* evaluation theory. Four of these components—programming, valuing, knowledge, and utilization—are discussed here in terms of their implications for CPE evaluation practice. The standards of program evaluation—accuracy, feasibility, propriety, and usefulness—intertwine at points with the components of evaluation theory and are discussed as such (Joint Committee on Standards for Educational Evaluation, 1994).

Figure 5.1 introduces the Situated Evaluation Framework (SEF) to anchor the discussion of the components of an evaluation theory specific to CPE. The framework situates the learner and knowledge assessment at the junction of the CPE educational context, the participant's practice context, and the evaluation context. Knowledge is processed—for example, transferred or negotiated—by the learner between the educational and practice contexts. The educational context influences the learner through program process and content as well as program planning. The practice context influences the learner through organizational facilitators and social support. How knowledge is understood and assessed depends on the nature of the influencing contexts, learner characteristics, and theories-in-use. The assessment of knowledge may focus on its

Figure 5.1. Model of Learning in CPE

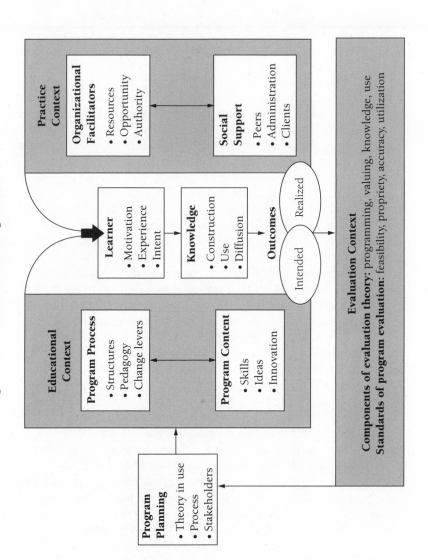

construction, use, diffusion, or some combination thereof. For example, some participants may diffuse CPE knowledge to others without using it in their own practice. Evaluation enters the CPE educational context through program planning and gathers data from both the educational and the practice contexts to assess realized CPE outcomes, both intended and unintended. Outcomes realized in practice inform future or ongoing CPE program planning.

The theoretical components of effective CPE evaluation theory include programming, valuing, knowledge, and utilization. Table 5.1 presents these components in terms of questions and examples in evaluation practice.

CPE Programming Theory. Programming theory attends to a couple of deceptively simple questions. What is the CPE *program*? How is it intended to work? Program theories—no matter how formal or informal—give clues about program boundaries and the feasibility of intended outcomes. For example, in evaluating a one-day CPE program in substance abuse prevention, the use of citywide measures of substance abuse reduction were abandoned for more proximal measures of change, such as postprogram activities of participants (Ottoson, 1996). Such measures would have been both infeasible and unfair evidence of CPE's effects in the given circumstances. To help define what constitutes a CPE program, the following areas are adapted from evaluation theory (Shadish, Cook, and Leviton, 1991): adult learning theory, internal program process and content, and external facilitators and support.

Adult Learning Theory. CPE programming theory needs to rest on what we know about how adults learn. "Each educational program, then, makes a statement about the way the world ought to be" (Cervero and Wilson, 1994, p. 5). This program statement shapes not only the planning of CPE but also what the CPE evaluation will focus on and when and how it will do so. Different adult learning theories might be used in the SEF to link the education and practice contexts. For example, transfer of learning theory might be used to determine whether the skills taught in the CPE program are moved intact from the educational to the practice context. A successful program outcome would be a skill used in practice that looks the same as the one taught in the CPE program. To achieve success from a transfer perspective, the CPE process would include elements such as sufficient practice time or comparable practice and educational environments (Baldwin and Ford, 1988).

In contrast, situated cognition theory might be used in the SEF to explore the interaction among the educational context, the participants' experience, and the practice context. A successful program outcome would be ideas or skills situated—adapted, evolved, or abandoned—in context rather than transferred wholesale. To achieve success, the CPE process would incorporate opportunities for critical reflection (Lave and Wenger, 1991). Using situated cognition theory, CPE evaluation would seek evidence of critical reflection, not sufficient practice time. The point here is not to advocate for one theory or another but rather to insist that CPE evaluation account for the learning theory used.

Internal Program Components. The programming component of evaluation theory needs to account for internal program process and content as

Table 5.1. Components of CPE Evaluation Theory and Related Practice Questions

Theory Component	Evaluation Practice Questions	Examples
Programming *What is the CPE program? How is it intended to work?*	What learning theory is used?	Transfer, situation cognition, diffusion, social learning
	What are the internal program planning, process, and content?	Program boundaries, administrative structure, objectives, methods, skills taught
	What are the levels for program change?	Person, process (planning), resource use, timing
	Which external factors influence the program and application of learning?	Competing priorities, sufficient resources, support from others, power role
Valuing *What is the basis for determining CPE value? Who decides?*	What is the evaluation logic? Is it transparent?	Criteria, standards, performance
	What are the outcome criteria?	Behavior change, reflection, client services, cost savings
	What are the process criteria?	Characteristics of the educational and practice contexts
	Who is included (excluded) in criteria selection?	Educator, employer, client participant, public
	Are values prescribed or described?	What CPE outcomes ought to be vs. what outcomes occur
Knowledge *How is knowledge about CPE value constructed?*	What counts as real evidence of CPE success?	Stories, numbers, money demonstrations, journals
	Does evidence vary by stakeholder?	Policymaker, educator, client employer, public, participant
	What trade-offs are made among evaluation standards?	Accuracy, feasability, propriety, utility
Utilization *Are evaluation findings used? By whom? Toward what ends?*	Which kinds of CPE evaluation use are acceptable?	Improve program, punish, market, publish, cut funding
	What is CPE evaluation use?	Instrumental vs. conceptual
	What is the use time frame?	Immediate vs. eventually
	How actively does the evaluator encourage use?	Plan for use, actively encourage use, hope for use

well as the program planning that shaped them. In CPE evaluation, program process includes internal organizational structures as well as pedagogy, instructional plans, program formats, schedules, resources, location, marketing, teaching strategies, and administration (Caffarella, 1994). The nature of the program content, or what participants are to engage in practice—skill, ideas, or innovations—influences evaluation methodology and findings. For example, program content that is compatible with existing practice is more likely to be applied than content that is incompatible (Rogers, 1995).

An analysis of these components and their presumed linkages to outcomes shape CPE evaluation questions. Is there a program to evaluate or merely a collection of components? When does the program begin or end? Are the intended learners the same as program participants? Such basic questions of program theory are critical to CPE evaluation. Of what value is it to focus on the outcomes of a CPE program if we have no idea what the program is and can never reproduce it or know enough about it to let others build on its success? CPE programming theory clarifies the *program* to be evaluated.

The Change Process. If one of the reasons for doing CPE evaluation is to improve programs, then it is important to make explicit the ways in which such programs change. What are the levers for program change embedded in program process? Does change occur incrementally or radically? If a program occurs one time, how are evaluation results intended for use in the planning of future programs? Is it even possible to change the program at all or is it rigidly cast in stone by structures or personalities? How will the results of the evaluation be used to effect program change? The implementation literature proves helpful in understanding the change process (Ottoson and Green, 1987) and how program managers use information to effect change.

External Program Influences. CPE programs do not operate in a vacuum. Evaluation needs to consider the context of programs to help explain whether and how intended CPE outcomes are achieved. The context includes competing economic, political, social, and professional interests. Programming theory helps sort out on what basis the CPE evaluation attends to or ignores these different interests. At a minimum, three levels of context surround CPE. At the micro level is the educational context, in which there are immediate pressures, such as program implementation or CPE provider viability. At the meso or intermediate level is the practice context within which CPE participants engage and continue their learning. As the SEF indicates, facilitators and support at this level include organizational characteristics, such as sufficient resources or administrative and peer support to engage learning. At the macro level, which encompasses both the educational and the practice contexts, are concerns about the public good and the contributions that the professions and education for them make to it. If the ideas of CPE programs are to be realized in practice, CPE evaluation needs to be situated in a broad understanding of context. At the very least, CPE evaluation needs to assess elements of the practice context and their effect on the engagement of learning in practice. Without consideration of such factors, it is difficult to know if some programs fail because of the programs themselves or because of the inhospitable environment to which some CPE participants return.

CPE Valuing Theory. Evaluation concerns itself with assessing value. "This element of judgment against criteria is basic to evaluation and differentiates it from many other kinds of research" (Weiss, 1998, p. 15). Early CPE evaluations judged success against criteria, such as participant satisfaction. Current evaluations suggest that behavioral change and client or patient impact are the best criteria to judge CPE success. Does this mean that a CPE program is effective because it leads to behavioral change in practice? Is it ineffective because behavioral change did not occur? A wide range of economic, administrative, professional, personal, political, social, and organizational criteria can be used to focus evaluation and judge CPE value (Patton, 1997). Various levels of organization have been used to connect different kinds of criteria. For example, Kirkpatrick's (1975) widely used levels of training outcomes—reaction, learning, behavior, and results—were later expanded by Cervero (1988) to fit the CPE context. In the complex environment of CPE evaluation, it is no small task to negotiate criteria, levels, and stakeholders. The valuing component highlights the core valuing questions: On what basis will the value of CPE programs be determined? Who decides?

A valuing theory seeks to make answers to these questions transparent through an understanding of the steps in evaluation logic: determine criteria, set standards, and measure performance (Scriven, 1980). These steps link to Mager's (1975) objective-setting questions: What will change? By how much? By when? Under what conditions? Criteria used to judge CPE value include satisfaction, behavior change, or cost savings. Control of evaluation is exercised in these criteria, which may be embedded in the programming theory in use or in stakeholder agendas in the practice context. CPE evaluation theory needs to make transparent how these criteria are accessed.

It is not enough to make CPE criteria transparent, however. It is also necessary to make transparent the participatory or exclusionary process of their construction. A valuing theory seeks to move questions about CPE value beyond the technical process of writing objectives to the social and political process by which criteria are determined. Who gets to decide by which criteria CPE value will be judged? Educators? Participants? Professions? Employers? Society? Different stakeholders have different purposes for CPE and therefore use different criteria to judge CPE value. For example, program managers may be interested in the effectiveness of the program, while educators may be interested in which teaching strategy works best. Is it possible to include the criteria of multiple stakeholders in the same CPE evaluation? Weiss (1998) cautions about trying to include all possible criteria and suggests that "the all-purpose evaluation is a myth" (p. 33). Making evaluation both transparent and participatory means making it clear which criteria determine CPE success and whose perspectives are included or excluded in making that judgment. CPE evaluation theory needs to account for multiple stakeholder perspectives as early as the planning process.

Valuing theory is also concerned with the prescriptive or descriptive nature of evaluation criteria. Descriptive criteria indicate what is; prescriptive criteria dictate what should be. Prescriptive criteria dictate what constitutes an effective CPE program. For example, a good CPE program should lead to behavioral change, networking, or satisfaction. Descriptive criteria, in contrast, indicate what is valued in the program. For example, the participants are satisfied with the teaching strategies. Some argue that whichever criteria are used, it is the evaluator's responsibility to synthesize evaluation findings and declare the program good or bad. Others would argue that such synthesis should come from the stakeholders, not from the evaluator. A theory of valuing needs to consider what works best for CPE evaluations and under what circumstances.

A valuing theory lays bare not only the criteria by which CPE success is judged, but also the process by how these criteria were determined. Outcomes and process criteria go hand in hand in evaluation and are connected to the programming theory in use. Translating evaluation language from "meeting objectives" to "valuing transparency" expands the conception of CPE evaluation from a technical process to the social, political, and economic process it is.

CPE Knowledge Theory. A theory of evaluation knowledge is concerned with how knowledge about the value of the CPE program is constructed. That is, how do we know the CPE program is successful? This potentially abstract question hit home with practical reality in a recent evaluation (Ottoson, 1996). Both quantitative and qualitative data were collected about the effects of CPE training in substance abuse prevention. When findings were reported, stakeholders responded diversely. Some examined the findings for every number, table, graph, and accompanying analysis in the report. They talked in numbers, they understood in numbers, and they wanted more numbers. Others who received the data thumbed over the numbers to get to the stories of participants' experiences during and after the training. For them, numbers were a distraction to understanding experience. These stakeholders accepted different methods and evidence as *real* indicators of CPE success (or failure).

Just as CPE evaluations have determined that there is no magic bullet in educational methodology (Oxman, Thomson, Davis, and Haynes, 1995), a theory of knowledge needs to remind us that there is no magic bullet in evaluation methodology. For different questions and stakeholders, different kinds of knowledge construction may be appropriate and count as real evidence. A theory of evaluation knowledge needs to focus on more than methods. It needs to consider more fundamental questions about the evaluator's stance and about what will count as real evidence of the intended or realized outcomes of CPE.

A look at the current summaries and meta-analyses in the CPE evaluation literature suggests that the only real knowledge we have about CPE outcomes is from quantitative studies. These findings are heavily influenced by the health professions and their traditionally positivist origins. Although such knowledge construction may well fit some of the health professions, it does not fit all professions or other kinds of CPE stakeholders. Has quantitative data and an objectivist stance become the default knowledge construction in CPE evaluation? If it has, then a theory of CPE evaluation needs to consider the kinds of questions to which CPE evaluation has limited itself.

As is indicated by the SEF (Figure 5.1), knowledge construction in CPE needs to be tempered with the four standards of program evaluation: accuracy, feasibility, propriety, and utility (Joint Committee on Standards for Educational Evaluation, 1994). Although all of these standards are directly applicable to CPE evaluation, it is the accuracy standard that is most closely tied to the construction of knowledge. This standard intends "to ensure that an evaluation will reveal and convey technically adequate information about the features that determine worth or merit of the program being evaluated" (p. 125). The accuracy standard is concerned with such issues as program documentation, context analysis, sources of information, validity and trustworthiness of data, and justified conclusions. Unlike research in which accuracy may be held as an absolute standard, the standards of program evaluation acknowledge the potential trade-offs among all standards that the practice of evaluation may require. What is technically accurate in CPE evaluation may need to be traded against what is feasible for and useful to stakeholders.

A theory of knowledge in CPE evaluation moves the discussion beyond methods to a more encompassing look at how knowledge is constructed and for whom it counts as real evidence of CPE success, and to an exploration of the practice trade-offs deemed necessary in arriving at CPE evaluation findings.

CPE Utilization Theory. Evaluation knowledge or findings are intended for use in actual practice. "Where basic research puts the emphasis on the production of knowledge and leaves its use to the natural processes of dissemination and application, evaluation starts out with use in mind" (Weiss, 1998, p. 15). So important is use to program evaluation that it is identified as both a standard for program evaluation and a component of program evaluation theory. The utilization component (Table 5.1) suggests that a theory of CPE evaluation use needs to consider such tricky issues as what constitutes use, a time frame for use, and the extent to which the CPE evaluator should actively engage in promoting use.

CPE evaluation can serve a number of different purposes. As discussed earlier, these differences in purpose not only shape the criteria stakeholders seek as evidence of CPE success, but also shape how stakeholders use that evidence. For example, educators may be interested in using CPE evaluation findings to improve the program, funders may use the findings to continue or cut the program, employers may use the findings to send or withhold future participants, and participants may use the findings to compare their experience with that of others. A theory of use in CPE evaluation needs to provide a justification for prioritizing among stakeholder purposes and intended uses. Some purposes are "above the table," such as improving programming or determining programming effectiveness; other purposes slip below the table, such as gathering data to remove someone from his or her job or scuttling an effective program that is no longer of political interest. A theory of use in CPE evaluation needs to consider acceptable and unacceptable purposes for CPE, especially in light of the evaluation standard of propriety. For example, the SEF (Figure 5.1) shows that the outcomes of CPE can be used to inform program planning through evaluation.

The use of knowledge generated by evaluation has been a concern in policy and program evaluation over time (Weiss, 1998; Patton, 1997). Little attention has been paid to this in the CPE evaluation literature, however. This lack of attention to evaluation use is ironic considering that educators are concerned about participant use of CPE learning in practice.

What constitutes use? In an instrumental understanding of use, evaluation findings are handed over to the intended stakeholder, who acts on the information in a relatively short period in a way consistent with the findings and attributable to them. An enlightened or conceptual understanding of evaluation use assumes a more circuitous route between findings and use, with intervening influences and with adaptations that make findings hard to recognize or trace. Whichever understanding of use one adopts, the follow-up question is, Whose responsibility is it? The approaches to use vary from the CPE evaluator pushing for and supervising CPE use to the evaluator handing over findings and hoping for the best. Whatever understanding and approach toward use of CPE evaluation findings is taken, these need to be built into the evaluation from the beginning. Evaluation use needs to be a forethought, not an afterthought.

Situating CPE Evaluation

It is not enough to do CPE evaluation. It is the thinking behind the doing that needs to be exposed to the light of day. A CPE theory of program evaluation seeks to make the evaluation processes transparent. Program evaluation theory enhances objective-based evaluation by linking intended processes with realized outcomes, both intended and unintended. Evaluation distinguishes itself from basic research with its program-derived questions (programming), judgmental quality (valuing), and applied knowledge (knowledge construction and utilization). CPE evaluation occurs in political and action contexts in which standards of feasibility, propriety, accuracy, and usefulness guide evaluation practice. The SEF introduced in this chapter attempts to account for the ways in which the CPE educational context and the participants' practice context interact in adult learning and inform future CPE programming through evaluation.

To move toward useful CPE evaluations, it is time for CPE to stop borrowing everyone else's theory and move toward a CPE evaluation theory of our own.

References

Baldwin, T. T., and Ford, J. K. "Transfer of Training: A Review and Directions for Future Research." *Personnel Psychology,* 1988, *41,* 63–105.

Caffarella, R. S. *Planning Programs for Adult Learners.* San Francisco: Jossey-Bass, 1994.

Cervero, R. M., and Wilson, A. L. *Planning Responsibly for Adult Education.* San Francisco: Jossey-Bass, 1994.

Cervero, R. M. *Effective Continuing Education for Professionals.* San Francisco: Jossey-Bass, 1988.

Davis, D. A., Thomson, M. A., Oxman, A. D., and Haynes, R. B. "Changing Physician Performance." *Journal of the American Medical Association,* 1995, 274(9), 700–705.

Joint Committee on Standards for Educational Evaluation. *The Program Evaluation Standards.* (2nd ed.) Thousand Oaks, Calif.: Sage, 1994.

Kirkpatrick, D. L. *Evaluating Training Programs.* Madison, Wisc.: American Society for Training and Development, 1975.

Lave, J., and Wenger, E. *Situated Learning: Legitimate Peripheral Participation.* Cambridge, Mass.: Cambridge University Press, 1991.

LeCompte, M. D., and Preissle, J. *Ethnography and Qualitative Design in Educational Research.* (2nd ed.) Orlando: Academic Press, 1993.

Lewin, K. "Field Theory Is Social Science." In D. Cartwright (ed.), *Problems of Research in Social Psychology.* New York: HarperCollins, 1951.

Mager, R. F. *Preparing Instructional Objectives.* Belmont, Calif.: Fearon, 1975.

Ottoson, J. M. *Training Evaluation Report of 1994–1995 Profile, Feedback, and Follow-Up Data.* Contract no. 277–91–2004 Rockville, Md.: United States Department of Health & Human Services, Substance Abuse and Mental Health Services Administration, Center for Substance Abuse Prevention, Division of Community Prevention and Training, Training and Evaluating Branch, 1996.

Ottoson, J. M., and Green, L. W. "Reconciling Concept and Context: A Theory of Implementation." *Advances in Health Education and Promotion,* 1987, *2,* 353–382.

Oxman, A. D., Thomson, M. A., Davis, D. A., and Haynes, B. R. "No Magic Bullets: A Systematic Review of 102 Trials to Improve Professional Practice." *Journal of the Canadian Medical Association,* 1995, *153*(10), 1423–1431.

Patton, M. Q. *Utilization-Focused Evaluation.* (3rd ed.) Thousand Oaks, Calif.: Sage, 1997.

Rogers, E. M. *Diffusion of Innovations.* (4th ed.) New York: Free Press, 1995.

Scriven, M. *The Logic of Evaluation.* Inverness, Calif.: Edgepress, 1980.

Shadish, W. R., Cook, T. D., and Leviton, L. C. *Foundations of Program Evaluation: Theories of Practice.* Thousand Oaks, Calif.: Sage, 1991.

Smith, J. K. *The Nature of Social and Educational Inquiry: Empiricism Versus Interpretation.* Norwood, N.J.: Ablex, 1989.

Umble, K. E., and Cervero, R. M. "Impact Studies in Continuing Professional Education for Health Professionals." *Evaluation & the Health Professions,* 1996, *19*(2), 148–174.

Waddell, D. L. "The Effects of Continuing Education on Nursing Practice." *Journal of Continuing Education in Nursing,* 1991, 22(3), 113–118.

Weiss, C. H. *Evaluation.* (2nd ed.) Englewood Cliffs, N.J.: Prentice Hall, 1998.

JUDITH M. OTTOSON is associate professor in the School of Policy Studies at Georgia State University in Atlanta, Georgia.

6

Effective marketing strategies can promote attendance, enhance the satisfaction of registrants, and help continuing professional education programs meet financial goals.

Marketing Realities in Continuing Professional Education

Ruth F. Craven, Martha B. DuHamel

"This is the best CE course I've ever been to!" "Thanks for a great day!" When comments like these are made about a conference with a capacity crowd and a balanced budget, the continuing professional education (CPE) provider has a marketing success. What role does marketing play in creating a successful conference? In most cases, the key role. Occasionally CPE providers are assured of full enrollment and a balanced budget because of training contracts, mandatory educational requirements, educational grants, special subsidies, and commercial underwriting. However, most CPE providers rely on marketing strategies to attract registrants. They make decisions about brochure design, size, color, and graphics. They agonize about whether the title will grab a reader's attention. Does the brochure have enough information? Too much information? Is the description of the target audience too broad? Too narrow? How many copies of the brochure should be printed? What mailing lists should be used? Is a specific journal ad worth the cost? When should the brochure be mailed out? Should it be mailed twice? Should more resources be devoted to marketing on the Web? Is the fee too high or too low? Is the keynote speaker a "draw"? Should lunch be included to enhance the appeal? For each educational offering, CPE providers make hundreds of programmatic decisions, which in effect are also marketing decisions.

Over the past decade, many organizations and institutions have reduced or eliminated subsidies of professional education programs. Without a financial safety net, many CPE programs have closed. Those that have survived are pedaling fast to balance their nonprofit missions with a mandate to be self-sustaining. Most CPE providers recognize that effective marketing is the

NEW DIRECTIONS FOR ADULT AND CONTINUING EDUCATION, no. 86, Summer 2000 © Jossey-Bass Publishers

key to survival, but they fear that their on-the-job, self-taught marketing skills may be inadequate for the challenge ahead. Many educators have never taken a marketing course. Those who have may have found Madison Avenue strategies and jargon difficult to apply to CPE.

However, times are changing and CPE marketing is becoming a more visible, well-researched field of its own. Innovative CPE providers are analyzing, labeling, and teaching about this niche of marketing. Elliott (1997) has wallpapered most CPE offices with his "Effective Seminar/Conference Marketing" brochures, and he entreats CPE providers to have a marketing plan that they evaluate and reevaluate continually. Shore (1999a) urges CPE providers to follow his commandments of strategic marketing. He warns, "Every year, CPE providers forget, ignore, or—worse yet—sabotage their programs by not knowing or not following key tenets of successful marketing" (p. 80).

Basic Principles of CPE Marketing

What are the key tenets of successful CPE marketing? Shore (1997, p. 80) identifies what he refers to as the Commandments of Strategic Marketing. He indicates that knowing the customer, hunting for a specific niche, communicating with customers, analyzing the competition, becoming a brand maker, making the right offer to the right people at the right time, exploring distribution channels, testing materials, and delivering on promises are all essential to effective CPE marketing.

To experienced CPE providers, these commandments are clever restatements of time-tested CPE dictums. The business jargon—*branding, market niche,* and *channels of distribution*—may be a bit foreign, but each tenet can be explained in more familiar CPE terminology. Here are nine corollaries to Shore's commandments:

1. *Identify your target audience.* In marketing your program, you must have a specific group of professionals in mind. Plan your programs for them, name them in your marketing materials, and send them direct-mail announcements and brochures. Individuals are more likely to register (and employers are more likely to support an employee's attendance) when they see their own profession named in promotional materials. Make it easy for them to register and attend. Remove such barriers as early bird discounts, late fees, and excessive cancellation fees. Provide maps, good directions, and a confirmation letter. Recognize their need for practical education with real-world applications. Treat them as valued customers whose opinions matter, because it is for their educational needs that your program exists.

2. *Define your mission.* Why are you offering CPE programs? What is your niche? Are you a fundraising arm of your organization? Is your mission to disseminate faculty research, provide postgraduate education for students, improve the public's health, recruit students for academic programs, foster a coalition of people with a common cause? Whatever your mission,

create a written document stating that mission and discuss it with everyone who has a vested interest in your program. Your mission will guide your decisions and actions. With it you will be able to identify specialty areas in which you can excel and audiences that your program is uniquely able to serve. Your mission will validate your existence in the eyes of colleagues, accrediting agencies, and administrators. "Successful marketing is first a state of mind, then a state of action" (Shore, 1997, p. 80).

3. *Assess the needs of your community.* Create an advisory committee made up of representatives from employers, community organizations, and subgroups of the professionals you serve. Get their input on the educational needs of their colleagues and on potential speakers. For each educational offering, invite selected members of the target audience to serve on a planning committee. Because volunteer time is scarce for most professionals, use the committee's time wisely by minimizing time spent on administrative details and maximizing time spent planning educational content and selecting credible speakers.

4. *Identify your competition.* Determine what sets your program apart from programs that target the same audience. Get to know your competitors. Who are they? What are their missions? When and where do they offer their programs? How much do they charge? How well do they meet their objectives? How do they market their offerings? Get on mailing lists that advertise to your audience. Read newsletters, newspapers, and journals for advertisements about other programs. Request and analyze brochures from your competitors. Check their Web sites. Register and attend their offerings. Talk with colleagues about their perceptions of your competitors' target audiences, quality of offerings, costs, and market niches.

Use what you learn to identify factors that distinguish your offerings from those of your competitors. Are you both useful but interchangeable commodities in the marketplace? If so, one of you may not be needed. However, if you have a unique identity—that is, a "brand"—use it to establish and strengthen your market niche and become more than a commodity in your field.

5. *Establish your credibility.* To develop a track record or a brand identity with your audience, become known for conducting well-run, high-quality programs in pleasant surroundings with helpful support staff and knowledgeable speakers. Find out what other characteristics your constituents value and seek to include them in your program. It is important to know who comes to your offerings, but what is more important is to know who comes back. Building a relationship with registrants has important spinoffs for both sides. Professionals who feel some ownership in your programs will contribute their expertise to the planning, use their influence to recruit new attendees, and make your work more enjoyable because of the collegial spirit that arises from these relationships.

6. *Develop a marketing plan.* For most CPE programs, the most useful strategies include (1) a calendar of courses mailed quarterly, semiannually, or annually to members of the target audience; (2) detailed course brochures

mailed directly to previous registrants and subgroups that are most likely to be interested in attending; (3) brochures sent in bulk to selected agencies for internal distribution; (4) announcements in newsletters, newspapers, and journals; (5) a Web site with your brochures on-line; and (6) e-mail announcements. Other options include postcards, letters of invitation, flyers displayed at other conferences and on bulletin boards, and public service TV and radio spots. CPE providers cringe when they hear, "I never heard about the program!" from a regular participant. Marketing research is available to help with decisions about using commercial mailing lists, selecting the size and color of brochures, timing your mailings, setting fees, and much more. However, be sure to look at your own track record. Analyze successes and failures and learn from them.

7. *Provide options.* Working professionals are pulled in many directions. Look for opportunities to offer content in different formats, such as creating independent study courses from live conferences, repeating courses in different locations, teleconferencing to multiple sites, distributing course manuals, or selling recordings of specific lectures. Consider offering university credit for an additional fee or working with other CPE providers to offer the same conference for different audiences. Providing options not only helps you educate more professionals but also increases revenue and strengthens the visibility of your program.

8. *Evaluate your program.* Course evaluations are your most important guide to successful future offerings. Invest the staff time needed to summarize evaluations. Use evaluations to identify effective instructors, document a successful track record for co-sponsors, improve support services, provide feedback to facilities, help new instructors improve, select topics for future conferences, and provide encouragement for staff and planning committee members to continue their efforts. Analyze data on the cost of planning, promoting, and conducting each offering. Determine what percentage of revenue was spent on marketing and which strategies yielded the best results. Create annual reports and compare results from year to year.

9. *Deliver quality programs.* "Service is not a competitive edge. It IS the competitive edge" (Elliott, 1997). If you provide detailed information in promotional materials, including learning objectives, content, benefits of attending, speaker credentials, the schedule of events, catering, parking, professional credit, and disability accommodations, both you and your participants will be much happier. By reducing the discrepancy between expectations and results, you will improve your credibility and strengthen your customer base. When problems arise, such as a speaker drops out at the last minute or audiovisual equipment fails, problem solve to the best of your ability, apologize, and make amends.

Learning from Colleagues

During the past decade, a number of individuals and organizations have taken the lead in identifying and researching marketing strategies for continuing professional education (Elliott, 1997; Shore, 1999a, 1999b). From their work, CPE providers are learning tricks of the trade that are useful in marketing decisions. Consider the following rules of thumb for times of indecision.

Pricing. When setting the price of an offering, use $45 and $95 as price points (Shore, 1999a). In other words, rather than charging $217, consider adjusting the price upwards to $245 or dropping back down to $195. The principle here is that the dollar amount of tuition is only one consideration for a potential participant. Other considerations include the total cost of attending, confidence in the provider, credibility of the program, and other benefits of attendance, for example, networking, reunion with colleagues, and mental stimulation. The bottom line is not to waste time worrying unnecessarily about the price, and not to set the tuition at a less-than-optimal or unrealistic level.

Cancellations. Learning Resources Network (LERN) (1999) suggests that having to cancel 10 to 20 percent of offerings because of underenrollment is ideal. In our experience, this is a high percentage, but some programs that advertise one offering in multiple locations may find that 20 percent of twenty locations is an acceptable figure if all are marketed on the same brochure. A rate closer to 0 to 5 percent is more desirable to maintain credibility as a dependable CPE provider. Canceling programs can contribute negatively to future marketing efforts, particularly when participants have to absorb prepaid travel costs or reschedule vacation and work schedules.

Offering new courses. When is a new course considered a winner? LERN says if you come within 10 percent of breaking even on direct expenses on a new program, you have a winner. This figure might make you feel better when a new course does not meet its budget, but a steady diet of such courses could be very hard on your program's budget.

Promotion expenses as percentage of income. LERN recommends that promotional expenses be approximately 20 percent of an offering's budget. To spend more than 25 percent is generally considered to be too high.

Response to direct mail advertising. According to Shore (1999a), a 1 to 10 percent return from your VIP group (that is, your most dependable group of repeat attendees) is a very good return on your marketing investment. In this sense, return means the number of registrations that are received as a result of direct mail marketing. When mailing brochures or marketing to an unfamiliar audience, the return tends to be under 1 percent. In our program at the University of Washington, return on mailed brochures is an average of 2 percent on the number printed, and higher if we only count the number mailed. For our VIP group, our return is about 8 percent.

Response time. For planning purposes, monitor the response rate at least weekly to help you estimate the number of registrants who will attend an offering. This will help you determine whether you need to switch to a larger or smaller room, negotiate a realistic catering contract, estimate the number of syllabi to print and when they need to be ordered, advise speakers about the makeup of the audience, and determine whether or not you can expect sufficient enrollment to hold the course.

To estimate enrollment, analyze your records and compare how many registrants you had at the same point from one year to the next. Determine the average point between when you mailed a brochure and the date by which half your registrants had responded. The figure will vary among audiences and specific offerings, but knowing patterns will simplify many decisions. Typically, when brochures are mailed out three months before an offering, half the audience will have registered four weeks before the event.

Repeat advertising. As the response trend becomes clear, LERN (1999) recommends spending more marketing resources on promotion for winners and less on losers. This is probably the opposite of what is done in many CPE programs.

The authors of this chapter look forward to more research and sharing among CPE providers about these tricks of the trade. During periods when offerings are well subscribed and budgets are in the black, rules of thumb tend to be taken with a grain of salt. However, when programs are under pressure to produce more offerings and charge higher fees, advice from colleagues is more likely to be sought and tested. Collegial interchange is as important for CPE providers as it is for the professionals they educate.

Self-Assessment for CPE programs

The following self-assessment may be helpful in analyzing the health of a CPE unit. For the questions to which you answer no, consider investigating the reasons and developing a strategy for correcting the problem. Time spent strategizing will pay off if you have a plan (and you will sleep better at night).

1. Is the budget in the black? Is there a comfortable balance (of perhaps, the equivalent of six months' operating expenses) with which to take risks in programming?
2. Is there enough well-trained staff and a well-equipped office for carrying out the functions required to conduct quality educational programs?
3. On average, are sufficient numbers of registrants attracted to courses to pay both direct and indirect expenses? If the program is subsidized in one way or another, is that subsidy secure or is there a need to become proactively self-sustaining?
4. Is the feedback from registrants positive? Do participants report that courses meet their objectives and expectations for attending?
5. Is there a supportive constituency? Is the umbrella organization supportive? What is the nature of relationships with other community organizations?
6. Is a mission statement written?
7. Is an advisory committee established?

8. Has our competition been identified?
9. Are annual reports prepared for the purpose of comparing trends and program strengths and weaknesses? Do the reports indicate what percentage of income is spent on promotion?
10. Are registrations tracked as they come in and are these data used to influence marketing decisions?

If you do not already keep track of the marketing plan for each offering, consider doing so. Keep it simple so that the task is not daunting. Include the number of brochures and other promotional materials printed, mailed, and distributed; lists used for mailing and e-mailing; publications in which ads were placed (including the contact person, cost, time lag between submission and publication); copies of each ad or brochure; a summary of the number, geographic origin, disciplines, and employers of registrants; problems with any of the strategies used; and the cost of promotion. Each year analyze your marketing strategies and look for trends. Discuss your data and hypotheses with coworkers and colleagues. Sharing your concerns with members of the CPE team who work on the front line and who plan the programs can be instructive for all concerned and can yield valuable insights and lead to new program initiatives.

Conclusion

The required benchmark of any CPE program is that it meets the educational needs of the professionals to whom offerings are directed. The interplay between quality educational planning, capable program administration, and insightful strategic marketing makes CPE a dynamic and challenging field. Success in one area enhances success in the others. The essential objective is to market offerings that are based on assessed educational needs, advocacy for each profession, and ultimately, benefit to the public.

References

Elliott, R. Effective Seminar/Conference Marketing." Clemson, S.C.: Clemson University, 1997.

Learning Resources Network. "Now It's Time to Gather End of Year Statistics: Report 1J28." [http://www.lern.org/members_area/common/library/reports/1j28.cfm] 1999.

Shore, D. "Shore's Commandments for Successful Marketing Strategies." *Medical Meetings,* Dec. 1997, pp. 80.

Shore, D. *Best Practices in Continuing Education for the Health Professions.* Cambridge, Mass.: Harvard Continuing Education Conference, 1999a.

Shore, D. "Developing and Building Your Brand." *Growing Your Business,* March/April 1999b, 5–7.

RUTH F. CRAVEN is professor in the Department of Biobehavioral Nursing and Health Systems and assistant dean for educational outreach in the School of Nursing at the University of Washington, Seattle.

MARTHA B. DUHAMEL is director of continuing nursing education at the School of Nursing, University of Washington, Seattle.

7

Continuing professional education practitioners work in environments where ethical problems surface and create dilemmas requiring hard decisions. Practical applications for ethical decision making are presented, providing practitioners with an ethical framework to enhance their professional practice.

Ethical Issues in Continuing Professional Education

Patricia Ann Lawler

Continuing professional education practitioners are challenged on many levels today in our work. As earlier chapters in this volume have shown, our roles and responsibilities cover a wide variety of disciplines, tasks, and obligations. We work in diverse settings—colleges and universities, professional associations, business and industry. We work with numerous constituencies, including the professions of medicine, accounting, education, allied health, and government, to name just a few. It is within these environments, with their varying social, cultural, and institutional conditions, that ethical problems surface and create dilemmas for us.

Here is a typical example. Alice Kinsley, program director for a prestigious university's continuing professional education division, found herself under increased pressure as her dean directed her to increase revenue by creating a certificate program in human service management. Alice realized that her university did not have the expertise or experience to offer a first-class accredited program, and that there were several institutions in her metropolitan area that already offered such a certificate. However, her dean insisted that the institution's name and reputation would sell the program and argued, "Just our name will get the participants jobs and promotions." Alice was caught between the financial needs of the university and her professional commitment to the welfare of her students.

Dilemmas in our professional life, such as the one Alice found herself in, often challenge us to review our goals and purposes. They also demand difficult and critical decisions and consideration of not only the environmental issues but also the many stakeholders who may be involved. All of our activities, such as evaluation, marketing, collaboration among providers, workplace learning, and professional practice, have ethical dimensions. Yet in our work we tend to be most concerned with getting the job done and working through our management problems. This perspective may preclude effective strategies for working with people within organizations and creating constructive and successful decisions. Using an ethical perspective to view conflicts and problems offers us an alternative decision-making strategy that can lead to improved professional practice. A clear understanding of the problems of continuing professional educators can ensure that important issues will not be overlooked and that adequate data, not just anecdotal evidence, will be utilized (Lawler and Fielder, 1993).

This chapter explores ethical problems inherent in continuing professional education. Within this context, ethical decision making can be seen from a variety of perspectives, and educators can begin to identify the issues that arise in their work. Utilizing a practical model with useful strategies that consider the rights and interests of the diverse stakeholders promotes ethical practice in continuing professional education. Finally, the personal and professional development of an ethical practitioner in continuing professional education is addressed.

Ethical Problems

Ethical problems arise when we are faced with questions about fairness and about obligations owed to our colleagues, customers, participants, and other stakeholders (Lawler and Fielder, 1993). Ethics sets limits regarding what people can do in pursuit of their own interests, and prescribes standards of behavior governing their dealings with others. Many organizations and most professions have developed formal codes of conduct and standards of practice to address typical problems that employees and practitioners encounter in their work.

Because of its interface with a variety of other professions and organizations, continuing professional education is subject to ethical problems that arise out of a conflict of values. The values and rules of conduct, written and unwritten, that are appropriate for one environment may not be valid when extended to another. The core values of continuing professional education represent the basic beliefs and goals of the profession, and there has been much discussion in the literature regarding the development of a code of ethics based on these values (Carlson, 1988; Connelly and Light, 1991; Lawler, 1996; Sork and Welock, 1992; Wood, 1996). For instance, CPE professionals ascribe to such values as respect for and advocacy of adult students, fair treatment of all persons associated with continuing professional education, and concerns for organizational and program integrity (Lawler and Fielder, 1993). However, these core values may, and likely will, differ from the core values and standards of conduct of the constituencies a continuing professional educator may serve. For example, including promotional material on financial advising in a presentation in a business environment would not raise any eyebrows, but it would be unethical for an instructor in a continuing education course at a university to do this. We have different obligations depending on whether we are dealing with colleagues, clients, customers, superiors, students, strangers, or patients. Because all of these groups participate in continuing professional education, and because ethical problems are inherent in much of what we do in planning for continuing professional education, sensitivity to ethical issues is essential (Imel, 1991; Lawler, 1998). Ethical sensitivity, the ability to identify ethical issues, assists us in recognizing these situations (Brockett, 1990; Cervero and Wilson, 1994; Lawler, 1998; Lawler and Fielder, 1993).

Continuing professional education is also subject to the kind of ethical problems that occur in any organization. Besides developing and delivering programs, most educators are also involved in routine organizational life. Ethical problems may include questionable administrative actions or inaction, unfair treatment of the less powerful, making exceptions to policies that unfairly favor a person or group, arbitrary application of policies for promotion or other rewards, creating program policies or standards that are discriminatory, financial misconduct, and conflicts of interest (Lawler and Fielder, 1993). Here, too, different constituencies may have different standards of conduct. For example, accountants have less autonomy and stricter regulations concerning disbursement of funds and record keeping than university administrators.

In addition to these aspects of ethics in continuing professional education, the field is undergoing significant changes. Cervero (Chapter One, this volume) identifies four trends affecting continuing professional education that will generate new ethical problems and require practitioners to develop appropriate standards of conduct. First, education offered at the workplace dwarfs all other forms of continuing education but also has received less scrutiny. Workplace education offers as many, if not more, opportunities for ethical dilemmas, such as violations of privacy, conflict of interest, exploitation of participants, and unfair application of policies for rewards and punishments, as a traditional educational setting. Second, distance education brings new ethical problems concerning the use of on-line resources, privacy, equitable access, intellectual property, new forms of cheating, and redefining the relationship between student and instructor. Third, collaboration between universities and companies requires that the rules for proper conduct in collaboration be examined because of the very different values and cultures each party brings to the relationship. For example, the large amounts of money to be made in CPE raise anew the old question of the fair allocation of continuing education income. Fourth, integrating continuing education into professional careers offers opportunities for manipulating standards for political reasons. Turf battles are part of professional life, and continuing education can be misused to exclude or weaken one's professional opponents through judicious selection of content, instructors, program design, and delivery. Those responsible for establishing benchmarks for credentials and certification have significant power over who and what provider may qualify for program approval.

In all of these ethical issues it is important to distinguish several different tasks. First, CPE professionals need to be sensitive to ethical issues in their work and not view them as simply another management problem. Ethics are concerned with treating people right, not just getting the job done. Second, CPE professionals need to adopt a systematic decision-making strategy for dealing with ethical problems (Brockett, 1988; Lawler and Fielder, 1991). As with any significant organizational problem, simply playing it by ear and finding ad hoc solutions may demoralize those affected and cause subsequent organizational problems. Third, professional societies in continuing education and other groups need to develop standards of conduct for the kinds of ethical problems typically encountered in a given area of practice. Recently the Association for Continuing Higher Education (ACHE) developed and adopted a code of ethics by conducting surveys of practitioners to identify typical problems, by identifying core professional values, and by finding consensus concerning the ethical guidelines that should be applied (Lawler, 1996). An understanding of these tasks facilitates the process of identifying ethical problems.

Identifying Ethical Problems

Identifying the ethical problems in our daily work as continuing professional educators requires more than a cursory knowledge of ethics or being familiar with ethical directives. It requires us to be aware of the underlying values of our profession, and of the cultural context and political issues inherent in organizational life. When a college or university contracts with a corporation, for instance, organizational differences can lead to ethical problems as these two diverse organizations, with their distinct missions and goals, come together to educate professionals. This diversity in values is not just an organizational phenomenon, however. As we perform our professional roles, our own value systems, goals, and experiences affect how we see a problem and respond to it (Hiemstra, 1988). Conflicts can arise between individuals and also between an individual and an organization, such as we saw with Alice at the beginning of the chapter. Since organizations demand allegiance and commitment to their goals and priorities, members of the organizations are required to meet their obligations, comply with rules and regulations, and adhere to the mission, goals, and policies of the organization (Lawler, 1996). This may create conflicts because one's goals and values may be in conflict with those of another person or the institution. For continuing education professionals this dilemma is often seen in the controversy over whether continuing education should be market driven or learner centered (Kerka, 1996). As practitioners, we may be caught between an institution's goal for fiscal success and profit, with its focus on what the market will bear, and a professional goal of meeting the learning needs of the participants. Kerka points out that we often seem obsessed with this fiscal success, which may harm the delivery of programs and the effectiveness of the learning. Like Alice, we may be caught between meeting the fiscal objectives that our role in the organization may require and feeling comfortable about the content and delivery of programs to meet our students' professional development needs (see Craven and DuHamel, Chapter Six, this volume).

These situations provide examples of conflicts between legitimate goals and values. As Burns and Roche (1988, p. 53) point out, "The practice of ethics is an exercise in clarifying the nature of conflicting claims." Ethical sensitivity is useful in examining conflicting perspectives. To increase ethical sensitivity, Zinn (1993) proposes that we ask ourselves a series of questions that would focus on the use of words we use to describe the situation, such as *right* or *wrong* and *fair*. Such questions would also cover violations of published codes, potential harm for various stakeholders, conflict of values, and whether or not one would feel comfortable taking the same action in a "clean, well-lit room." Zinn's questions conclude with, "Do I have a gut feeling that something is not quite 'right' about this?" (p. 8). First recognizing that the situation has an ethical dimension and that one is uncomfortable about the conflict provides an opportunity to begin an ethical decision-making process.

Ethical Decision Making

There are several ways we can go about making ethical decisions. First, we can be prepared for ethical dilemmas by being familiar with codes of ethics, codes of conduct, professional standards, and guidelines for practice. In continuing professional education this may mean understanding not only the codes and guides for those of us working with adult learners, but also the standards inherent in the professional content we are delivering. We can become familiar with ethical principles and situations in which ethical issues arise by reviewing such codes and standards across the professions. These guides can provide us with a starting point for considering the issue at hand. Professionals in the field of continuing education can turn to the Principles of Good Practice in Continuing Education developed by the Continuing Education Unit (Brockett, 1988), to ACHE's Code of Ethics (*ACHE Proceedings*, 1997), and to the Academy of Human Resource Development's proposed Standards on Ethics and Integrity (Kuchinke, 1999). Although Connelly and Light (1991) and Wood (1996) propose principles and frameworks for an ethical code, the continuing education profession has yet to establish a code of ethics.

Although such guidelines are helpful, we must also understand how our experiences, professional development, and value systems come into play. Hiemstra (1988) has proposed a second framework for ethical decision making that takes these elements into consideration. He recommends that we engage in an analysis of our personal values and philosophy to identify our own core value system. Our philosophy of education and our values regarding learners and education are the foundation of our practice. Understanding their influence and the impact they have on our decision making is crucial in making ethical decisions. Within this context we are able to assess our role responsibilities and those of other stakeholders in an ethical dilemma.

Finally, with knowledge of the professional standards and our own value system we can turn to taking action when engaged in an ethical dilemma. Because these dilemmas require action, we need to frame and analyze the situation in a systematic way. Many models have been proposed to aid the practitioner in working through ethical dilemmas (Lawler and Fielder, 1991: McLagan, 1989; Newman and Brown, 1996: Walker, 1993; Zinn, 1993). Many of these models propose a linear approach to decision making and rely on a problem-solving model. Lawler (1997) and Fielder (1996) provide us with a more helpful framework with which to consider ethical dilemmas. It proposes the following questions (pp. 243–244):

1. *What is the ethical question?* This locates the problem where the decision maker encounters it.
2. *What are the alternatives?* This step asks the decision maker to consider a number of different responses.
3. *What rules or principles should guide the choice of alternatives?* The strength of this model is that it focuses on articulating shared ethical rules as the basis for the decision.
4. *What personal or organizational goals are at stake?* Frequently there are conflicts between what is ethically required of us and what we want for our organization or ourselves. The ideal result in decision making is to find a way to meet all of our ethical obligations as well as other goals.
5. *Of all things considered—ethical obligations, other goals, and practical matters—what is the best alternative?* Decision making is ultimately a matter of striking a balance among conflicting demands. Although there is no formula for determining this balance, making the elements explicit and clarifying their importance will ensure that the important factors will be taken into consideration.

Improving Ethical Practice in Continuing Professional Education

Continuing professional educators work in environments where ethical problems surface and create dilemmas that require hard decisions. Because of the diversity of providers and organizations offering continuing professional education, issues and problems are constantly facing us in our work. This volume aptly addresses many of these challenges and provides a foundation for our own professional development. Continuing our own education and developing a greater awareness of ethical issues is inherent in becoming an ethical practitioner (Imel, 1991). Conversations among reflective practitioners should focus on ethical problems to identify and illustrate the ethical dimensions of our work and to develop ethical quidelines for our practice. Professional meetings and conferences are excellent opportunities for these conversations to occur both formally through workshops and sessions and informally over meals and in corridors. Brockett (1990) provides another suggestion for improving ethical practice. He recommends that we go beyond our own profession and examine how other professions deal with ethical issues. This is especially important for us as we deal with a wide variety of content areas and professions. Because many of us work with other professions in providing educational opportunities for doctors, accountants, and health care practitioners, to name only a few, we are presented with the opportunity to inquire into the core values and ethical guidelines inherent in these professions. Using these connections to explore core values, ethical issues, and obligations to stakeholders will enrich our own learning, increase our ethical sensitivity, and lead to the creation of successful programming.

Although ethical problems may appear daunting at times, the field of adult and continuing education has a long history of sensitivity to the various constituencies it serves. This history provides us with a foundation on which to build a strong ethical framework to guide our practice. The principles of adult and continuing education, which emphasize respect for learners and their needs and establishing suitable climates and programs, can guide our practice in the future (Lawler, 1991). As we meet the demands of the new millennium and future trends, we can rely on our past and on reflective practice to enhance our ethical approach to continuing professional education.

References

ACHE Proceedings. University Park, Pa.: Pennsylvania State University, Oct. 25–28, 1997.

Brockett, R. G. "Ethics and the Adult Educator." In R. G. Brockett (ed.), *Ethical Issues in Adult Education.* New York: Teachers College Press, 1988.

Brockett, R. G. "Adult Education: Are We Doing It Ethically?" *MPAEA Journal,* Fall 1990, pp. 5–12.

Burns, J. H., and Roche, G. A. "Marketing for Adult Educators: Some Ethical Questions." In R. G. Brockett (ed.), *Ethical Issues in Adult Education.* New York: Teachers College Press, 1988.

Carlson, R. A. "A Code of Ethics for Adult Education?" In R. G. Brockett (ed.), *Ethical Issues in Adult Education.* New York: Teachers College Press, 1988.

Cervero, R. M., and Wilson, A. L. *Planning Responsibly for Adult Education: A Guide to Negotiating Power and Interest.* San Francisco: Jossey-Bass, 1994.

Connelly, R. J., and Light, K. M. "An Interdisciplinary Code of Ethics for Adult Education." *Adult Education Quarterly,* 1991, *41*(4), 233–240.

Fielder, J. H. "A Framework for Ethical Decision Making." Unpublished manuscript. 1996. Villanova University, Villanova, Penn.

Hiemstra, R. "Translating Personal Values and Philosophy into Practical Action." In R. G. Brockett (ed.), *Ethical Issues in Adult Education.* New York: Teachers College Press, 1988.

Imel, S. *Ethical Practice in Adult Education.* Columbus: Clearinghouse on Adult, Career, and Vocational Education, Ohio State University, 1991. (ERIC Digest No. 116)

Kerka, S. *Continuing Education: Market Driven or Learner Centered?* Columbus: ERIC Clearinghouse on Adult, Career, and Vocational Education, Ohio State University, 1996. (ERIC Myths and Realities)

Kuchinke, K. P. (ed.). "Standards on Ethics and Integrity." In *Academy of Human Resource Development Conference Proceedings,* Mar. 3–7, 1999, Washington, D.C.

Lawler, P. A. *The Keys to Adult Learning: Theory and Practical Strategies.* Philadelphia: Research for Better Schools, 1991.

Lawler, P. A. "Developing a Code of Ethics: A Case Study Approach." *Journal of Continuing Higher Education,* 1996, *44*(3), 2–14.

Lawler, P. A. "The Ethics of Evaluating Training." In S. M. Brown and C. J. Seider (eds.), *Evaluating Corporate Training: Models and Issues.* Norwell, Mass.: Kluwer, 1997.

Lawler, P., and Fielder, J. "Analyzing Ethical Problems in Continuing Higher Education: A Model for Practical Use." *Journal of Continuing Higher Education,* 1991, *39*(2), 20–25.

Lawler, P., and Fielder, J. "Ethical Problems in Continuing Higher Education: Results of a Survey." *Journal of Continuing Higher Education,* 1993, *41*(1), 25–33.

McLagan, P. A. *Models for HRD Practice.* Alexandria, Va.: American Society for Training and Development, 1989.

Newman, D. L., and Brown, R. D. *Applied Ethics for Program Evaluation.* Thousand Oaks, Calif.: Sage, 1996.

Sork, T. J., and Welock, B. A. "Adult and Continuing Education Needs a Code of Ethics." In M. W. Galbraith and B. R. Sisco (eds.), *Confronting Controversies in Challenging Times: A Call for Action.* New Directions for Adult and Continuing Education, no. 54. San Francisco: Jossey-Bass, 1992.

Walker, K. "Values, Ethics and Ethical Decision Making." *Adult Learning,* Nov./Dec. 1993, pp. 13–14, 27.

Wood, G. S. "A Code of Ethics for All Adult Educators?" *Adult Learning,* Nov./Dec. 1996, pp. 13–14.

Zinn, L. M. "Do the Right Thing: Ethical Decision Making in Professional and Business Practice." *Adult Learning,* Nov./Dec. 1993, pp. 7–8.

PATRICIA ANN LAWLER *is associate professor in the Center for Education, Widener University, Chester, Pennsylvania.*

8

Professionals' traditional expertise and authority are increasingly being eroded by the demands of the institutional delivery systems in which they routinely practice. Consequently, they are increasingly unable to address clients' needs responsibly.

Professional Practice in the Modern World

Arthur L. Wilson

To begin—a story. I have arrived a few minutes early for my appointment because there are always many others scheduled for the same time. From experience I know that where my name is on the sign-in list determines (although not predictably) when I might actually be seen by the professional. Of course the gatekeeping ritual of verifying who I am, that I am indeed scheduled for this time, and all importantly, whether I have presented the right sets of identifier numbers to ensure that I have the means to finance my appointment also determines my place in line. If I successfully negotiate this first interaction with the receiving clerk who controls access to the examining spaces, I then settle in to wait. I always bring work with me, although waiting rooms, with their incessant buzz of people and patients, are not at all conducive to doing much except waiting. As I work, I spend much of my time eyeing the staccato scurrying of technical assistants in order to judge who might next pass into the examining sanctum and where I am in that invisible queue.

Once escorted through the doors, I begin a succession of encounters with the professional's assistants, each of whom requires me to move to some new part of the office warren so that I might be tested, measured, certified, and so on. Finally ensconced in an examining space, I am visited by an assistant who performs many monitoring tasks, codes results onto forms, and typically asks for some generalized symptomatic statement for why I might be needing "service." Once "charted" and having heard the clunk of the clipboard dropping into the chart box on the door, I again settle into waiting.

I know the professional is about to enter the process when the clipboard leaves its door holder. A knock typically follows a flutter of page flipping. Pleasantries are followed by a review of the symptomatic reason for the visit, a quick exam that typically confirms the assistants' speculations, more charting, rarely time for questions, maybe prescriptions and tactical advice, and then the professional is gone. I can usually count on the professional's part to be the briefest of the many encounters. Once "treated" I typically pass back through some segment of the technical assistants I first encountered, but I always terminate with a visit to the payment window. Thus concludes my "treatment."

It's the System!

I am, of course, describing my experience in a health care delivery system. Not at all fictionalized, my description presents what I take to be routine courses of events and patterns of interaction in the world of "modern" professional practice, a scenario that most participants have come to take for granted as normal. Lest I be accused of unfairly singling out the medical system, there are clearly many other examples that follow essentially the same scenario (law, education, military, government). Recall your last interaction with nearly any modern professional system—a similar scene is likely.

That I describe no faces is no accident. The images of system delivery I portray here clearly contradict cultural icons of individualized professional competence and care as evidenced by smiling health care workers on billboards or advocacy lawyers on television. Although I ultimately argue that people are truly responsible for what happens to us in these professional systems, it is just as clear to me that professionals too often are letting the system do their thinking and acting for them. My starting point is that individual professionals no longer treat individuals; systems do. How we understand this modern world of systemic professional practice clearly shapes how we are treated as beneficiaries of professional services, how we act as professionals in these systems, and how we, as continuing educators, respond to the education needs and demands of professionals as learners. This chapter describes the effect of the systemic institutional conditions shaping professional practice at the turn of this century and begins to think constructively about how we as continuing educators might responsibly respond to the learning needs of professionals whose practices both shape and are shaped by the systems in which they work.

The Conditions of Professional Practice

The question of context has not gone unaddressed in the discussion among continuing educators about how these conditions shape both practice and continuing education. Houle (1980) had a sense of the significance of context in his depictions of professionalization and lifespan learning. But it is clearly Schön's (1983) image of the reflective practitioner that embedded practice in the real world of actual work. That is, in "naming" the practice problems before them, professional practitioners have to "talk" to the situation, for it is the situation that shapes what the professional might do. Cervero (1988, 1992) and

Nowlen (1988) ended the 1980s with significant texts that addressed the question of context head on. Cervero captured the essential tension of contextualized professional practice—"wise action"—as the best action in a specific context within a specified ethical framework. Nowlen clearly depicted the professional intricately bound up in a "double helix" of professional performance as profoundly shaped by individual ability within complex organizational and cultural circumstances.

The 1990s saw the question about the conditions of practice continue to be of concern, but in many ways the responses become less sociologically sophisticated. Curry and Wergin's (1993) edited volume contains certain insights, among which McGuire's (1993) are the most prescient. In describing professional context, McGuire discusses significant trends leading to the systemization depicted earlier: the knowledge explosion and the concomitant increase of professional subspecialization; the rapid emergence of technology and its effect on the creation and storage of knowledge, and the increasing speed and (sometimes) democraticizing of access; the profound sociocultural changes of professional collegiality shifting to open marketing and competitiveness for client bases, and professional entrepneurialism shifting to organizational employment; and the rapid replacement of professional self-regulation with state mandated regulation. Queeney (1996, 1997) adds to the discussion by depicting competent practice as problem-solving ability in practice settings defined by technology, teams, and systems orientation. Together, McGuire's and Queeney's analyses point directly to the central sociological trend: increasing systemization of professional practice and service. Cervero (1998) rejoins the conversation to argue that rapid social change, knowledge proliferation, technology, and increasing provider cooperation all need to be understood in terms of who is benefiting from this complex interplay of professional practice and continuing professional education—and importantly, whose interests should be served but are not. In a time of rapid, almost rabid market and delivery systemization, such questions become critical. All of these discussions provide important responses to the question of how context shapes professional practice, but they fail to capture the complex relations among them. Although conducting such an analysis is too large an effort for this chapter, there are two effects we can begin to examine. First, missing is an understanding of how the systemization of the delivery of professional service is profoundly undermining professionals' abilities to practice effectively, specifically by limiting their professional power. Second, diminishing power leads to a loss of client advocacy in the face of growing systemization.

Practice in the Modern World: Expert Systems and the Loss of Certainty

The hallmark of professional acuity since the turn of the previous century has been the notion of professional discretionary judgment (Flexner, 1915). Historically we have presumed a social contract with professionals in which we trust them to care for our well-being. Professionals thus exercise "extraordinary power" and we trust them to use their expertise in our interests (Schön, 1983). My view is that increasing systemization of professional delivery is rapidly eroding these extraordinary powers, leaving an altered image of modern professional practice. I only begin to unpack two facets and their effects here: the growth of expert systems and the loss of professional certainty.

Growth of Expert Systems. No one can easily doubt the nearly complete demise of single practitioner offices in the professional world. As others have asserted (McGuire, 1993; Nowlen, 1988; Queeney, 1996), professional services today are most typically delivered systemically, not by individual practitioners working largely autonomously in the community. Corporations have replaced partnerships. But what is the nature of this systemic delivery? Giddens (1990, p. 27) terms them "expert systems" by which he means "systems of technical accomplishment or professional expertise." This is decidedly not just a reference to computerized decision-making systems. For Giddens, expert systems represent the large-scale organization and delivery of professional services based on a factory model (health management organizations, corporate law offices, government agencies, and so on). Recall the opening scenario with its assembly-line approach to professional service. And as Queeney (1997) notes, the notion of system competency is rapidly replacing our traditional notion of individual professional competency. Thus systemization of professional delivery is rapidly shifting dependency on practitioners to dependency on systems.

As such expert systems increasingly deliver professional services, certain sociological conditions become pronounced. First is a significant change in the character of social interaction between professionals and the people to whom they provide service. In classical client-professional relations, a degree of trust developed that depended on a continuing face-to-face commitment (Giddens, 1990). But systemic delivery undermines what Giddens calls *facework commitment*: "in modern social life many people, much of the time, interact with others who are strangers to them" (p. 80). This is no more evident than in participation in large professional delivery systems in which professional relations are defined by such things as access, availability, funding sources, and specialization rather than by ongoing face-to-face social interaction with people we know. Thus, as we have learned to expect in the modern world, systemization leads directly to depersonalization.

Second, as Giddens asks, "Why do most people, most of the time, trust in practices and social mechanisms about which their own technical knowledge is slight or nonexistent?" (1990, p. 88). Systemized depersonalization and clients' trusting ignorance conflate to increase what is already a relationship of dependency between client and professional. As Foucault (1977) has routinely shown in psychiatry, prisons, medicine, the military, and education, the result of the development of expert knowledge has produced relations of dependency by objectifying individuals as arrays of symptoms rather than as humans with needs. The result is that professionals increasingly have power to say who clients are and what is to be done with them, while clients are increasingly losing their abilities to counteract that exercise of power. That power, traditionally the reserve of individual professionals and a function of individual discretionary judgment, is now rapidly being colonized by the systems in which individual professionals participate; it is now the systems, not individual professionals, who decide what clients need and how they will be served. Thus independent professionals, who once had the power to make such determinations, are now caught up in structures that have usurped that power. The result? The loss of professional discretionary judgment. Although professionals typically still exercise expertise, they increasingly have less control over its use.

So, in my view the aggregation of professional service into large-scale delivery systems leads directly to the loss of power for both professionals and clients. Such systems depersonalize client-professional relations, which reduces the ability of clients to participate in their own treatment. That depersonalization is a function of the loss of discretionary professional judgment in which professionals are less able to use their expertise to serve client needs. Therefore, we must question whose interests are being served (Cervero, 1998) and how the systemization of delivery shapes even the best of intentions.

Risk and the Loss of Certainty in Professional Practice. Schön (1983) has sought to shake us out of the complacency of century-old ideas about what constitutes professional practice. In the conventional understanding, science is the basis of sound professional practice in which the professional practitioner is trained to recognize predictable problems and apply reliable remedies (Larson, 1977; Schön, 1983). Schön's now classic depiction of the "crisis in professional knowledge" resulted from the interaction of two significant forces. First, a rapidly complexifying society of interrelated problems resists easy codification and reliable solutions (Beck, Giddens, and Lash, 1994). Second, scientifically derived professional knowledge remains ill-suited to remedy ongoing practical problems (Cervero, 1988; Schön, 1983; Wilson and Hayes, forthcoming). That crisis has not diminished; indeed, it is increasing.

One reason for the quickening of that crisis is the emerging awareness that we live in what Beck, Giddens, and Lash (1994) termed a *risk society,* which they describe as the "phase of modern society in which the social, political, economic and individual risks increasingly tend to escape the institutions for monitoring and protection in industrial society" (p. 5). They argue that as we develop expert systems to respond to complexifying society and its problems, a paradox arises: "the more we try to colonize the future, the more likely it is to spring surprises on us" (p. 58). Agricultural experts increase crop productivity; environmental experts demonstrate resulting land, air, and water degradation. Educational experts increase test scores as industrial experts demonstrate an ignorant workforce dangerous to itself and society. Health care is increasingly managed to reduce costs and generate profits; consumer advocates demonstrate that fewer people receive health care. In each example, and countless others, there are always professional experts ready to stake their expertise on predicting certain outcomes. But the point is that we are not able to calculate precisely the risks of such professional interventions (the premise of technical rational knowledge and professional practice) and are able to array only scenarios whose likeliness depends on unpredictable, often unrecognized conditions. The result is that we "are being expected to live with a broad variety of different, mutually contradictory, global and personal risks" (p. 7).

The important observation this analysis offers is to show that the very thing our traditional notions of professional ability were to resolve has now returned to the center of our modern lives. Professional expertise was to remove uncertainty from life, to "colonize the future" by using expert knowledge to define and control our lives. Now we must recognize (as sociologists have for a century) that attempts at controlling human phenomena directly contribute to increasing uncertainty—and thus the loss of certainty in professional life. What Schön originally depicted as a failure of professional "knowing" is really a more complex interplay of growing social tension in which the very systems we create to serve us increase the problems they are meant to solve. The growth of expert systems is leading paradoxically to the growth of risk and the loss of certainty.

Here in brief is my understanding of the contemporary conditions of modern professional practice. The autonomy of the individual professional expert, as traditionally based on professional knowledge and skill, is being superseded and undermined by the growing dominance of expert systems. As Giddens (1990) argues, expert systems depend on social trust that presumes that both clients and experts are beneficiaries of the systemic organization of professional expertise. Such systems, however, simultaneously create relations of power and dependency for both clients and professional practitioners (Foucault, 1977). Clients trust professional practitioners to act in the clients' interests, but professionals' power to do so is being eroded by the dominance of the professional systems in which they work (hospitals owned by insurance companies, corporate law offices headed by state legislators, and government regulators working for industrial political action committees, for instance). This process is occurring in a "risk society" (Beck, Giddens, and Lash, 1994) in which the now decades-old "crisis in professional knowledge" (Schön, 1983) is coupled with declining professional autonomy, competing and contradictory expert claims to knowledge, and the increasing inability of expert systems to respond effectively to the social conditions for which they were created. Such conditions produce a loss of certainty in professional action. My main point is that such systemization has decreased professionals' discretionary judgments, thus lessening their power, and they have responded by accepting less responsibility for the welfare of clients by deferring to the mechanization of the system whose interests often run counter to the provision of client benefits.

Prudent Action and Continuing Professional Education

In response to Nowlen's (1988) depiction of the individual's performance in a systemic and professional culture, I want to refine the conditions as ones of dwindling professional autonomy (literally a loss of power), increasing but perhaps misplaced organizational fealty, and a corresponding loss of advocacy for client well-being. As continuing educators, how should we respond? In response to this quickening context of risk and uncertainty, I propose building on Cervero's (1988, 1992) concept of wise action in order to develop an understanding of professional practice as prudent action (Wilson and Hayes, forthcoming) in which practitioners are responsible for representing their clients' interests in the unequal relations of power produced in an expert system context. Continuing professional educators must take a direct role in reshaping these relations of dependency. The problem is that too much traditional continuing professional education, with its emphasis on knowledge and technique updates, fails to understand the professional in this complex systemic context. To respond, we have to take a stance on, first, whose interests professionals should represent (Cervero, 1998), and second, whose interests we as continuing educators should represent. I take it as essential that we represent the interests of clients by helping professionals deal with their systemic loss of power and the failure of client advocacy. The role, then, of the continuing educator is to help the professional see that essential responsibility.

Continuing educators have three responsibilities in this regard. First, there is no doubt in my mind that most continuing professional education will continue its traditional function of facilitating the delivery of knowledge and technique updates. Queeney's (1997) recent comments, however, offer some interesting implications for continuing education. Although she stays wedded to a competency model of CPE, she opens up the possibility of referring to educators as performance analysts rather than just technical program deliverers. Nowlen (1988) of course introduced this view some time ago (see Mott, Chapter Three, this volume). Adopting a performance analysis stance increases our responsibility as educators in constructing continuing professional development. In analyzing performance we must take pains to show professionals how the encroachment of expert systems and the loss of certainty have undermined their traditional bases of power and altered their sense of responsibility.

Second, continuing educators must change their dominant understanding of what professionals need to be educated about in order to practice effectively. To do that we must fundamentally reorganize our understanding of what constitutes professional practice. The theory of and evidence for the "reflective practice" approach to continuing education is well established. Yet we remain mired in update and competency approaches. If we as continuing educators are to be effective, we must be able to develop continuing education that addresses the fundamental nature of professional practice, which we know now to be technically, politically, and ethically ambiguous rather than well understood and procedural. To do that we must promote learning from practice (see Daley, Chapter Four, this volume) rather than learning for practice, as Cervero (1988) introduced more than a decade ago and Jarvis (1999) has recently commented on extensively.

Finally, we must take a clear stance on whose interests really matter (Cervero and Wilson, 1994). Despite our organizational allegiances and economic bottom lines, our concern with ongoing collegial and competitive relations among providers, our fascination with delivery technology, and our obsession with program delivery facilitation, I believe our primary responsibility is to represent the interests of professionals in understanding and responding to the conditions I have outlined here. Professionals are constantly caught up in producing and reproducing the institutional and social mechanisms by which they operate, which in my view is leading to their increasing loss of professional autonomy and corresponding organizational rather than client allegiance. My sense is that most individual practitioners practice in good faith that they are indeed serving clients' interests well. My analysis here suggests that systemically that is not the case. Therefore, as educators, it is our responsibility to help practitioners see that and to redirect those changing relationships.

Conclusion

The practice of continuing professional education is of course caught up in the same dynamics I have sketched here and it must also deal with its own versions of these forces. Although traditional CPE has delivered effective responses to some important aspects of improving professional competency, it has for too long misunderstood the essential conditions of professional practice and what actual professional practice is really like. Until we reframe how we understand context and practice, we will contribute to our own diminishing power.

References

Beck, U., Giddens, A., and Lash, S. *Reflexive Modernization: Politics, Tradition and Aesthetics in the Modern Social Order.* Stanford, Calif.: Stanford University Press, 1994.

Cervero, R. M. *Effective Continuing Education for Professionals.* San Francisco: Jossey-Bass, 1988.

Cervero, R. M. "Professional Practice, Learning, and Continuing Education: An Integrated Perspective." *International Journal of Lifelong Education,* 1992, *11*(2), 91–101.

Cervero, R. M. "Continuing Professional Education in Transition." Keynote speech at the Symposium on Workplace Learning and Performance in the Twenty-First Century, University of Alberta, Institute for Professional Development, Edmonton, Alberta, Canada 1998.

Cervero, R. M., and Wilson, A. L. *Planning Responsibly for Adult Education.* San Francisco: Jossey-Bass, 1994.

Curry, L., Wergin, J., and Associates. *Educating Professionals.* San Francisco: Jossey-Bass, 1993.

Flexner, A. "Is Social Work a Profession?" *School and Society,* 1915, *1,* 901–911.

Foucault, M. *Power/Knowledge: Selected Interviews and Other Writings, 1972–1977* (Colin Gordon, ed.). New York: Pantheon, 1977.

Giddens, A. *The Consequences of Modernity.* Stanford, Calif.: Stanford University Press, 1990.

Houle, C. *Continuing Education in the Professions.* San Francisco: Jossey-Bass, 1980.

Jarvis, P. *The Practitioner-Researcher: Developing Theory from Practice.* San Francisco: Jossey-Bass, 1999.

Larson, M. *The Rise of Professionalism.* Berkeley: University of California Press, 1977.

McGuire, C. "Sociocultural Changes Affecting Professions and Professionals." In L. Curry, J. Wergin, and Associates, *Educating Professionals.* San Francisco: Jossey-Bass, 1993.

Nowlen, P. *A New Approach to Continuing Education for Business and the Professions.* Old Tappan, N.J.: Macmillan, 1988.

Queeney, D. "Continuing Professional Education." In R. Craig (ed.), *ASTD Training and Development Handbook.* New York: McGraw-Hill, 1996.

Queeney, D. "Redefining Competency from a Systems Perspective for the 21st Century." *Continuing Higher Education Review,* 1997, *61,* 3–11.

Schön, D. *The Reflective Practitioner.* New York: Basic Books, 1983.

Wilson, A., and Hayes, E. "*Vade Mecum:* On Thought and Action in Adult and Continuing Education." In A. Wilson and E. Hayes (eds.), *Handbook 2000—Adult and Continuing Education: The Profession, Its Common Concerns, and Its Practices.* San Francisco: Jossey-Bass and the American Association for Adult and Continuing Education, forthcoming.

ARTHUR L. WILSON *is associate professor of adult education, Department of Education, Cornell University, Ithaca, New York.*

9

This chapter advocates reframing the vision of continuing professional education so that improvement of professional practice is at the core of services—services that would include market-driven product lines in education, evaluation, and consultation.

Continuing Professional Education: From Vision to Reality

Barbara J. Daley, Vivian W. Mott

The overall purpose of this volume has been to initiate an analysis and discussion of the current nature and scope of continuing professional education (CPE) in the United States, and to raise awareness of the trends and issues that will continue to affect the field in the new millennium. CPE is being influenced by changes in our society, workplace, professional practice, and preprofessional education, as well by as changes in learning theory, evaluation practice, and ethical responsibilities. The chapter authors in this volume have outlined trends affecting CPE; discussed the continuum of preprofessional and continuing professional education; analyzed learning and professional practice in the modern world, including the workplace; proposed new systems for learning and evaluation; outlined significant shifts in the market realities of CPE; and finally, correlated ethical decisions with trends in CPE.

A review of these chapters has led us to ask some difficult questions about the practice of continuing professional education. The first question we raise is, *What business are we in?* What do we as providers of continuing education do day in and day out? The second question we raise is, *How do we create new systems that foster continuing professional education, knowledge construction, collaboration, and authentic situated evaluation within the constraints of the current marketplace?* Can we develop the ideas advanced in this volume within the economic constraints that CPE providers face? Finally, we ask, *Is this just an academic discussion of continuing professional education or can we fundamentally reshape the practice of continuing professional education?* This final chapter conceptualizes our response to these questions and offers our suggestions for reframing the vision and mission of CPE.

NEW DIRECTIONS FOR ADULT AND CONTINUING EDUCATION, no. 86, Summer 2000 © Jossey-Bass Publishers

Reframing the Vision

We believe that one of the major changes needed within continuing professional education is a reformulated vision of our practice. We are not proposing just another exercise of placing vision, mission, and value statements on paper, never to look at them again. Rather, we are proposing a fundamental shift in the vision, mission, and purpose of our work as CPE providers. Wheatley (1994) examines the connections between vision and field theory, noting how visions can be seen as energy fields that "more closely resemble an ocean, filled with interpenetrating influences and invisible structures that connect. This is a much richer portrait of the universe; in the field world, there are potentials for action everywhere, anywhere two fields meet" (p. 51). We are proposing that the vision of CPE be expanded so that the field of continuing professional education and the field of professional practice connect to create the energy that Wheatley describes.

Thus we propose that within the field of CPE we should shift our approach from providing educational programs to improving the quality of client outcomes within the professions. By advocating this shift, we maintain that education is only one aspect of the improvement of professional practice. Brown and Elfenbein (1991) argue, for instance, that it is the "practitioner's ability to learn from practice in a contextual and reiterative way and then transfer that understanding into new knowledge that is both rigorous and relevant for practice" (p. 59) that offers the greatest hope for continuing professional education. This shift to a more integral and practice-centered role for CPE will propel the CPE provider into other areas of professional practice development and greatly expand the value of CPE for the practitioner. This is something that we as educators have been hesitant to embrace as a vision for CPE; yet because the ultimate purpose of providing education to professionals is to improve the delivery of services to clients, such a vision is at the very heart of our practice in continuing professional education.

Cervero and Wilson (Chapters One and Eight, respectively, this volume) both address the issue of enhanced client services. Cervero indicates that the overall role of CPE is to improve professional practice; Wilson describes how "prudent action" in CPE represents the clients' interests in the unequal power relationships produced. If we shift our purpose and vision so that a stronger connection with the work of the professions is developed, we then fundamentally open our CPE practice to entirely new ways of thinking and acting. If we frame this issue as understanding what business we are in, we come to realize that our business is more than planning workshops, more than contracting with speakers, more than making sure the food service and hotel arrangements work. Rather, our business *should be* the identification of problems in professional practice and the determination of how education can foster professional development programs that ultimately promote the ability to work in the uncertain, confusing, and dynamic world of professional practice for the betterment of clients.

Wheatley (1994) provides a summary of why the creation of vision is so important to the work of CPE: "We need, therefore, to be very serious about this work of field creation, because fields give form to our words. If we have not bothered to create a field of vision that is coherent and sincere, people will encounter other fields, the ones we have created unintentionally or casually" (p. 56).

As Wilson indicates in Chapter Eight of this volume, the emphasis on expert systems and the loss of certainty in our modern world has in some ways already created other or unintentional fields of vision for CPE. By reframing our vision of CPE, the energy created in the process can move the practice of CPE to another level.

Creating the Reality

The question still exists, How can we create systems of learning, as Cervero discussed in Chapter One, that will foster improvement of professional practice? How can we continue to link preprofessional preparation with continuing professional education as Knox (Chapter Two) and Mott (Chapter Three) each proposed? One possible means would be by restructuring traditional continuing education provider units as Centers for the Advancement of the Professional Practice. We envision these centers as more than just the educational arm of professional associations or universities, but rather as the location of a multitude of services designed to foster the development of professional expertise and professional learning communities. As Eraut (1994) indicates, "the barriers to practice–centered knowledge creation and development . . . are most likely to be overcome if higher education is prepared to extend its role from that of creator and transmitter of generalizable knowledge to that of enhancing the knowledge creation capacities of individuals and professional communities" (p. 57). We are proposing that a reframed vision of CPE could lead to the creation of Centers for the Advancement of Professional Practice that offer to subscribers market-driven product lines in education, evaluation, and consultation.

Centers for the Advancement of the Professional Practice

In our vision of CPE, we see provider systems that are able to offer a variety of services to practitioners. Realistically, the type of center that we are proposing must be self-supporting, functioning as funded self-sustainable units. Gone are the days when CPE providers can rely on income generated by a parent unit for funding. Agencies employing professionals or individual professionals themselves could subscribe to such centers for services, with varying subscription rates and cafeteria-like services selection that would fit individual practitioner or agency needs. The selection of services could change on an annual basis as the needs of the subscriber changed.

The current trend of employers outsourcing educational services will very likely continue, thus putting the CPE provider in a position to generate new and significant amounts of business. The services of such a center could include education, evaluation, and consultation. Lest we be chastised for the prescriptive nature of these ideas, the examples developed here are meant to be illustrative rather than inclusive.

Education. Within these Centers for the Advancement of Professional Practice, the focus of educational delivery would necessarily be expanded. No longer would didactic, update presentations be the education focus. That is, even expertise would be reconceptualized as more than technical skill, the application of theory or principles, critical analysis, or even wise, deliberate action (Kennedy, 1987). Rather, professional development programs would be offered that have as their goals the improvement of the quality of professional services, brought about through the integration of authentic, situated, and practice-centered learning into the context of actual practice. New formats of educational delivery such as institutes and networking forums could be created. Institutes could provide education for new roles within the profession. Networking forums could afford professionals the opportunity to discuss and analyze practice patterns and service outcomes in their work environments. Additionally, to ensure authentic learning situated in practice, each education offering would include a follow-up or implementation component. That is, part of the educational service would be on-site consultation and follow-up to assist with the utilization of information in the practice arena.

Such implementation models already exist in some professions. Darling-Hammond and McLaughlin (1995, p. 598), for instance, describe a model for "new institutional arrangements called the Professional Development Schools (PDS)" for teacher preparatory and in-service or continuing education. According to these authors, to "create new structures for . . . learning, the usual notions of training and dissemination must be replaced by possibilities for knowledge sharing anchored in problems of practice" (p. 599). In many PDSs, for instance, university faculty, master supervising teachers, teacher-mentors, and newly licensed teachers work together on challenges encountered in the classroom, action research and evaluation projects, and ultimate redesign of preservice and in-service curricula. As Darling-Hammond and McLaughlin explain, such CPE programs actually create *communities of practice* that support professionals in dialogue and collaborative inquiry, encourage practice-based and practice-sensitive research, and foster the development of professional expertise and improved practice in the profession, thus enhancing both work and learning.

Another example may be found in continuing education programs for nursing in the United States. In a statewide program to educate staff in long-term care facilities on the mechanisms for implementing and managing dementia-specific care units, program planners included follow-up on-site consultation as part of the program. The program presenters and researchers were available to CPE participants to assist in setting up dementia specific care units at their long-term care facilities following attendance at the program. Thus, not only was the information on the establishment of the units presented, but educators worked in the practice arena to improve the delivery of services to clients by actively assisting in the establishment of more units based on the education provided (Kovach, 1997). In this fashion, the implementation component was tightly linked to the evaluation and consultation product line, as might be the case within the Centers for the Advancement of Professional Practice.

Finally, paper manuscripts, newsletters, and electronic communications could be created from educational offerings and be available to subscribers in multiple formats. Thus the education service would be expanded from traditional program provision to an additional service of continually providing new and up-to-date information in multiple forms.

Evaluation. Evaluation of professional processes and outcomes could be a major service of the centers envisioned here. Evaluation research could lead to the identification of practice problems and issues and thus support the identification of new education or consultation services that such centers could offer. But more importantly, as Ottoson notes in Chapter Five, this type of evaluation could also serve as the cornerstone for the improvement of professional practice. Ottoson outlines a Situated Evaluation Framework that, if used as intended, could pull together data from educational and practice contexts to demonstrate how knowledge was used in practice to reach the intended outcomes. This model would then provide data for additional practice development and program planning.

Data management could be a component of this evaluation service as well. Process and outcome data could be collected from multiple subscribers and stored in a regional database to serve as a benchmark comparison for the professional activities of subscribers. These benchmarks would allow subscribers to compare their agencies with an external database for accreditation processes and the overall improvement of professional quality. CPE providers have not traditionally thought of themselves as evaluators, but by expanding the CPE role to include this type of situated evaluation, we are moved closer to the vision of improving professional practice.

Consultation. Consultation services organized to improve professional practice and recreate professional systems could be offered by the centers as well. Consultation could be offered in the form of faculty practice (in a university setting) or independent consultation in other settings. For example, university-based faculty could establish joint appointments with practice agencies, thus facilitating the link between CPE programs and practice. The main issue here is that consultation not only increases the likelihood that ideas from CPE programs are incorporated into practice, but it also offers CPE providers a closer link with the practice arena, thus promoting an indepth understanding of both the facilitators and barriers to improvement of professional practice that exist across multiple contexts.

Conclusion

If, as Cervero (1992) and others point out, the goal of professional practice is wise and prudent action, then what may be needed is a new model of CPE. We advocate not only such a new model but a significantly expanded role for the CPE provider as well—a role in keeping with one of Houle's (1980) recommendations for the future of CPE. Houle suggests that the future vision of CPE would best be served only if continuing education were "considered as part of an entire process of learning that continues through the lifespan" (p. 308). We envision the CPE provider as the boundary spanner between continuing education and professional practice, with a clearly defined vision of the CPE role being the further development of professional expertise and the consequent improvement of professional practice. This places the CPE provider in a greatly expanded role, which necessitates the development of skills in education, evaluation, and consultation. The linking of education, evaluation, and consultation has the potential to "create an interconnected web of relationships in which the interactive processes [of CPE and professional practice] depend on one another for the growth and sustainability" (Lambert and others, 1995, p. 135) of providing professional services to clients. Such a web of mutually beneficial relationships will promote the responsibility and promise of CPE well into the new millennium.

References

Brown, S. M., and Elfenbein, M. H. "Experiential Learning: Reflection on Practice and the Organizational Action Scientist." Paper presented at the Eleventh National Conference on Alternative and External Degree Programs for Adults, Mobile, Alabama, Oct. 1991.

Cervero, R. M. "Professional Practice, Learning, and Continuing Education: An Integrated Perspective." *International Journal of Lifelong Education*, 1992, *11*(2), 91–101.

Darling-Hammond, L., and McLaughlin, M. W. "Policies That Support Professional Development in an Era of Reform." *Phi Delta Kappan*, April 1995, 597–604.

Eraut, M. *Developing Professional Knowledge and Competence.* Bristol, Pa.: Falmer Press, 1994.

Houle, C. O. *Continuing Learning in the Professions.* San Francisco: Jossey-Bass, 1980.

Kennedy, M. M. "Inexact Sciences: Professional Education and the Development of Expertise." *Review of Research in Education*, 1987, *14*, 133–167.

Kovach, C. *Late-Stage Dementia Care: A Basic Guide.* Washington, D.C.: Taylor and Francis, 1997.

Lambert, L., Walker, D., Zimmerman, D., Cooper, J., Lambert, M., Gardner, M., and Ford-Slack, P. J. *The Constructivist Leader.* New York: Teachers College Press, 1995.

Wheatley, M. J. *Leadership and the New Science: Learning About Organization from an Orderly Universe.* San Francisco: Berrett-Koehler, 1994.

BARBARA J. DALEY *is assistant professor in the Department of Administrative Leadership at the University of Wisconsin–Milwaukee.*

VIVIAN W. MOTT *is assistant professor in the Department of Counselor and Adult Education at East Carolina University, Greenville, North Carolina.*

INDEX

Back Issue/Subscription Order Form

Copy or detach and send to:
Jossey-Bass Publishers, 350 Sansome Street, San Francisco CA 94104-1342

Call or fax toll free!
Phone 888-378-2537 6AM-5PM PST; Fax 800-605-2665

Back issues: Please send me the following issues at $23 each.
(Important: please include series initials and issue number, such as ACE78.)

1. ACE _____

_____

_____

$ _____ Total for single issues

$ _____ Shipping charges (for single issues *only;* subscriptions are exempt from shipping charges): Up to $30, add $5^{50} • $30^{01}–$50, add $6^{50} $50^{01}–$75, add $8 • $75^{01}–$100, add $10 • $100^{01}–$150, add $12 Over $150, call for shipping charge.

Subscriptions   Please ❑ start   ❑ renew my subscription to *New Directions for Adult and Continuing Education* for the year _____ at the following rate:

U.S.:	❑ Individual $58	❑ Institutional $104
Canada:	❑ Individual $83	❑ Institutional $129
All Others:	❑ Individual $88	❑ Institutional $134

NOTE: Subscriptions are quarterly, and are for the calendar year only. Subscriptions begin with the Spring issue of the year indicated above.

$ _____ Total single issues and subscriptions (Add appropriate sales tax for your state for single issues. No sales tax on U.S. subscriptions. Canadian residents, add GST for subscriptions and single issues.)

❑ Payment enclosed (U.S. check or money order only)

❑ VISA, MC, AmEx, Discover Card #_____ Exp. date_____

Signature _____ Day phone _____

❑ Bill me (U.S. institutional orders only. Purchase order required.)

Purchase order #_____

Federal Tax I.D. 135593032   GST 89102-8052

Name _____

Address _____

Phone_____ E-mail _____

For more information about Jossey-Bass Publishers, visit our Web site at:
www.josseybass.com   **PRIORITY CODE = ND1**